Science for Potters

Science for Potters

Linda Bloomfield

Published by
The American Ceramic Society
550 Polaris Parkway, Suite 510
Westerville, Ohio 43082 USA

The American Ceramic Society
550 Polaris Pkwy., Suite 510
Westerville, OH 43082

© 2017, Reprinted 2018, 2020, 2021, 2024 The American Ceramic Society, All rights reserved.

ISBN: 978-1-57498-384-5 (Paperback)
ISBN: 978-1-57498-593-1 (PDF)

No part of this book may be reproduced, stored in a retrieval system or transmitted in any form or by any means, electronic, mechanical, photocopying, microfilming, recording or otherwise, without written permission from the publisher, except by a reviewer, who may quote brief passages in review.

Authorization to photocopy for internal or personal use beyond the limits of Sections 107 and 108 of the U.S. Copyright Law is granted by The American Ceramic Society, provided that the appropriate fee is paid directly to the Copyright Clearance Center, Inc., 222 Rosewood Drive, Danvers, MA 01923 USA, www.copyright.com. Prior to photocopying items for educational classroom use, please contact Copyright Clearance Center, Inc. This consent does not extend to copyright items for general distribution or for advertising or promotional purposes or to republishing items in whole or in part in any work in any format. Requests for special photocopying permission and reprint requests should be directed to Director, Publications, The American Ceramic Society, 550 Polaris Parkway, Suite 510, Westerville, Ohio 43082 USA.

Every effort has been made to ensure that all the information in this book is accurate. Due to differing conditions, equipment, tools, and individual skills, the publisher cannot be responsible for any injuries, losses, and other damages that may result from the use of the information in this book. Final determination of the suitability of any information, procedure or product for use contemplated by any user, and the manner of that use, is the sole responsibility of the user. This book is intended for informational purposes only.

The views, opinions and findings contained in this book are those of the author. The publishers, editors, reviewers and author assume no responsibility or liability for errors or any consequences arising from the use of the information contained herein. Registered names and trademarks, etc., used in this publication, even without specific indication thereof, are not to be considered unprotected by the law. Mention of trade names of commercial products does not constitute endorsement or recommendation for use by the publishers, editors or authors.

Publisher: Bill Janeri
Editor: Holly Goring
Technical Reviewer: Dave Finkelnburg
Design and Graphic Production: Boismier John Design, Columbus, Ohio

Cover image: Kate Malone's *A Pair of Summer Rain Atomic Bottles*, crystalline glazed stoneware, to 11 in. (28 cm) in height, 2014. *Image: Courtesy of Adrian Sassoon, London.*

Frontispiece: Stephen Parry's vase, 10 in. (25 cm) in height, stoneware, pine-ash glaze, wood fired, 2013. *Image: Courtesy of the artist.*

Acknowledgements

Thank you to my parents Susan and Michael Hart, for making sure I received an education in science. Thanks to Henry Bloomfield for constructing diagrams, proof reading, and making useful comments, and to Elin Barrett for the crystal lattice diagrams. Thank you to geologist Jonathan Phillips for help in identifying rocks. Many thanks to Holly Goring, Forrest Sincoff Gard, and Ash Neukamm of The American Ceramic Society for support in publishing the book and to Dave Finkelnburg for his edits and suggestions. Thank you to Sherman Hall for commissioning the book.

Many thanks to the potters who provided images: Matthew Blakely, Craig Edwards, Avril Farley, Matt Fiske, Mirka Golden-Hann, Tanya Gomez, Charlotte Jones, Heather Knight, Jan Lewin-Cadogan, Susanne Lukács-Ringel, Stephen Parry, Bjarni Sigurdsson, and Emma Williams. Thank you to Adrian Sassoon for the Kate Malone image and to the James Hutton Institute for the beautiful micrograph of kaolin. Thanks to Potclays for photographs of their clay pit at Brownhills and to John Doble for allowing me to visit his clay pit in Cornwall.

Table of Contents

Acknowledgements v
Introduction x

Chapter 1. Chemistry for Potters 1
    Elements 2
    Structure of the Atom 2
    Symbols 3
    Molecules 4
    Naming Compounds 5
    Bonding 5
    Crystal Structure:
        Cubic, Hexagonal, Close Packed, Spinel, Zircon 7
    Mohs' Scale of Hardness 12
    Color in Glazes 13
    Stains 18
    The Chemistry of Color 18
    Orbitals 18
    Crystal Field Theory 20
    The Potter's Periodic Table 21
    Metals and Non-Metals 23
    Trends Across a Period 24
    Trends Down a Group 25
    Metals 25
        Group 1 The Alkali Metals 25
        Group 2 The Alkaline Earths 26
    The Transition Metals 27
    The Rare Earths 28
    Poor Metals 29
    Semi-Metals 30
    Non-Metals 31

Chapter 2. Geology for Potters 36
    Rocks 37
    Geological Timescale 44
    Old Rocks: Precambrian to Devonian 45
    Coal and Fireclay: Carboniferous Period 45

Matthew Blakely's *Dartmoor Granite Sphere*, 7 in. (18 cm) in height, wood fired. *Image: Courtesy of the artist.*

Feldspar Formation	48
Bentonite and Stoneware: Cretaceous Period	49
The Great Extinction	49
Ball Clays	51
Glacial Clays	51
Minerals	51
Feldspar	53
Variants of Feldspar	55
Calcium	55
Magnesium	55
Barium and Strontium	57
Zinc	57
Boron	57
Silica	58
Alumina	58
Coloring Oxides Minerals	59
Opacifiers	63
US/UK Material Substitutions	65

Chapter 3. Clay 67
Types of Clay	67
Clay Bodies: Stoneware, Porcelain, Earthenware	72
The Structure, Properties, and Chemistry of Clay	75

Chapter 4. Glaze 81
Components of a Glaze	81
Eutectic, Phase Diagrams	82
Structure of a Glaze	85

Chapter 5. Glaze Formula 89
How to Calculate a Glaze Material Substitution	90
Material Substitutions	92
What Makes a Stable Glaze	93
Hardness and Scratch Resistance	93
Limits for Stable Glazes	94

Chapter 6. Glaze Fit 97
Silica Phases	97
Quartz and Cristobalite Inversions	97

    Glaze Faults and How to Correct Them 98
        Crazing. 98
        Shivering. 99
        Crawling. 100
        Pinholes 101
        Blisters 101
    Special Effect Glazes 102
        Matte 102
        Crystalline 103
        Chun 104
        Shrink and Crawl 106
        Volcanic 106
        Luster 107

Chapter 7. Glaze Additives 110
    Flocculation: Charged Particles. 110

Chapter 8. Firing 113
    Ceramic Change 113
    Kilns 114
    Measuring Temperature 116
    Oxidation and Reduction 117
    Wood and Salt 117
    Ash 120
    Conclusion 122

Bibliography. 125
Glossary 127
Appendices 131
    Appendix 1 Ceramic Materials List. 131
    Appendix 2 Orton Pyrometric Cone Temperatures. 134
    Appendix 3 Phase Diagram for Silica-Alumina-Calcia . . .135
    Appendix 4 Materials Analysis for US Frits, Clays, and
        Feldspars. 136
    Appendix 5 Materials Analysis for UK Frits, Clays, and
        Feldspars. 137
    Appendix 6 Complete Periodic Table of Elements 138

Index 140

Introduction

"I have tried in this book to build some kind of bridge between the territory of science and that of art. The bridge-builder's position is always an uncomfortable one, apt to be shot at from both sides. Artist potters will tell me that talking about atoms will not help anyone to make better pots, though personally I think it is as likely as any other study to help potters in that elusive pursuit. Bridge-building may be risky work, but somebody has got to do it because the need is great."

Michael Cardew, in Pioneer Pottery, 1969

It is almost half a century since Michael Cardew wrote about science in his book, Pioneer Pottery. Since then, more has been discovered about the structure of clays, geology and the origin of the Earth, as well as the structure of atoms and the sub-atomic particles inside them.

Unlike many potters, who typically train at art school, I trained as a scientist. I am therefore interested in the science of ceramics, particularly the chemistry of glazes and how colors are made. I believe artists should know where their materials come from and how they are formed. I also believe that this understanding gives potters additional insights into and additional freedom within the creative process. I hope this book will help potters understand more about the science of ceramics and that this understanding will allow them to develop their craft in new ways.

Linda Bloomfield, 2017

Jan Lewin-Cadogan's stoneware bowl, 6 in. (16 cm) in diameter, barium turquoise and lava glaze, fired to 2281°F (1255 °C) in oxidation, 2015. *Image: Courtesy of the artist.*

Salt fired porcelain by Susanne Lukács-Ringel, Germany, 2011. *Image: Courtesy of the artist.*

CHAPTER 1

Chemistry for Potters

Many potters come from an art background. When I taught my first glaze course in a college I was surprised to learn that some of my students had not learned any chemistry at school. This chapter will explain the basics of chemistry in clear and simple terms, including the elements, how they combine together to make compounds, and how they can form crystals. The form and structure of a crystal can affect its properties such as hardness and color, and can be useful in understanding the nature of clays and glazes.

The periodic table of elements is important in understanding how the elements are ordered into metals and non-metals. In ceramics, it is important to understand why metal oxides are basic or alkaline, non-metal oxides are acidic and how those oxides react together during firing.

Defining the Terms

Acid: A non-metal oxide which, when dissolved in water, releases hydrogen ions H^+. It will react with and neutralize an alkali or base.

Alkali: The oxide of an alkali metal or alkaline earth metal which, when dissolved in water, releases hydroxide ions OH^-. It will react with and neutralize acids.

Amphoteric: Able to act either as an acid or as a base/alkali.

Atom: The smallest unit of matter.

Base: A metal oxide which does not dissolve in water but will react with an acid.

Covalent Bonding: When atoms bond together by sharing electrons.

Electron: Small, negatively-charged particle inside the atom.*

Element: A single type of atom.

Ion: An atom or molecule which has lost or gained an electron.

Ionic bonding: When atoms bond by transferring electrons from one to the other.

Molecule: Two or more atoms bonded together.

Neutron: Particle in the nucleus of the atom which has no charge.*

Orbitals: Regions in which electrons of a particular energy are located around the nucleus.

Oxide: An element bound to oxygen.

Proton: Positively charged particle in the nucleus of the atom.*

Transition Metal: Element or ion with an incomplete inner electron shell.

Valence: The combining power of an element. The number of hydrogen atoms it will combine with.

*Atoms of heavy elements have more electrons, protons, and neutrons than atoms of lighter elements.

Elements

All matter is made from atoms. Atoms come in various types, which are called elements. The different elements, and the different ways they can be combined, produce the diversity of matter we see around us. The elements were forged in nuclear furnaces inside stars. Ordinary stars like the sun consume hydrogen as their fuel. Two hydrogen atoms are fused together to make a helium atom and, in this reaction, energy is released in the form of heat and light. Some larger stars are much hotter and helium atoms can fuse together to form heavier elements, such as carbon, oxygen, silicon, and iron, which is very stable. Elements heavier than iron, such as lead and uranium, are only formed when a massive star explodes to become a supernova. The dust left from the explosion eventually re-forms to make new stars and planets like our Earth. We are all literally made of stardust.

In the ancient world, the elements, or basic constituents of matter, were believed to be earth, air, fire, and water. We now know that there are in fact more than 90 naturally occurring elements, including metals, semi-metals, and non-metals. At ambient temperature, some elements exist as gases (e.g. oxygen), a few as liquids (e.g. mercury), and many as solids (e.g. iron), but their state of matter can change with temperature and pressure. As potters, we are most interested in the elements in the Earth's crust which form rocks, as these are also the elements present in clay and glazes. The most abundant are oxygen, silicon, and aluminium, followed by iron, calcium, sodium, potassium, and magnesium (1-1).

Structure of the Atom

Atoms were once thought to be the smallest units of matter, but we now know they are made up of a number of smaller, subatomic particles. In the center of each atom is the nucleus, which is a cluster of positively charged protons and neutrons, the latter having no electrical charge. Around the central nucleus there is a cloud of electrons, arranged in shells containing orbitals like planets in the solar system. However, the electrons vibrate very fast and not all the orbitals are spherical; some are in the shape of a figure of eight. The electrons in the outermost shell have the highest energy and are able to interact with other atoms. This interaction can cause atoms to bond together into molecules. The electrons are negatively charged and are attracted to the positively charged protons in the nucleus. In each atom, there are usually the same number of electrons as protons so that the overall electrical charge is zero. The number of protons is called the atomic number and is different for each element. The hydrogen atom has only one proton and one electron, while oxygen has 8 protons, 8 neutrons, and 8 electrons and silicon has 14

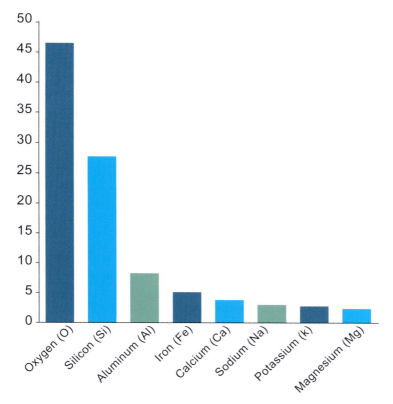

1-1. Bar chart of most abundant elements in the Earth's crust by percentage of the total weight. *Image: Henry Bloomfield.*

protons, 14 neutrons, and 14 electrons (1-2). The electrons are arranged in shells, each with a different energy level. The inner shell has 2 electrons, the next can hold 8, the next can hold up to 18, and so on.

Symbols

The elements each have a symbol, a single capital letter (B=boron) or two letters (Si=silicon). Some of the symbols for elements which were known in ancient times, come from Latin names, such as Sn, stannum for tin (connected to "stagnum", for pool, as it melts easily), and Cu, cuprum, for copper (the Latin name for Cyprus, where the metal was mined). Na comes from natron, the ancient Egyptian word for sodium. Other names and symbols were made up as each new element was discovered, often derived from Greek or Latin words, such as O for oxygen (Greek for acid producer). The latest elements to be discovered were synthesized in nuclear reactors and often named after a scientist or laboratory, e.g. Einsteinium is the element with atomic number 99.

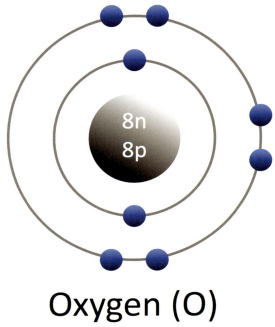

1-2. Oxygen atom, showing 8 electrons and a nucleus with 8 protons and 8 neutrons.

Molecules

The two most common elements in the Earth's crust are oxygen and silicon. When silicon bonds with oxygen it forms silicon dioxide, also known as silica, the main constituent of flint, quartz, and sand. It is not surprising that these two elements should also be found in many rocks and minerals, known as silicates. When a third element, aluminium, is added, the resulting mineral is called an alumino-silicate. Clays and feldspars are both types of alumino-silicates, containing silicon, aluminium, and oxygen.

When two atoms bond together, a molecule is formed. This happens either when two similar atoms such as oxygen bond to form O_2 gas or when different elements such as hydrogen and oxygen bond to form water, H_2O. Notice that, in writing down the formula for a molecule, we write the number of atoms of each element in that molecule.

Naming Compounds

Compounds are named using simple conventions. Compounds with two oxygen atoms are named "dioxide," for example, silicon dioxide. This can also be simplified to silica. An "a" on the end, as in silica, means combined with oxygen. An "ate" on the end, as in carbonate, means combined with both carbon and oxygen, or in silicate, combined with both silicon and oxygen. Some compounds are known by several names, for example, lime (as in limestone) is another name for calcium oxide. The names sometimes get more complicated, for example, iron sesquioxide means it has two atoms of iron to every three atoms of oxygen, written as Fe_2O_3, and also known to potters as red iron oxide. Lead sesquisilicate means two molecules of lead oxide to every three molecules of silica (or one lead to one and a half silica). This is also written as $2PbO \cdot 3SiO_2$.

Bonding

Only the electrons in the outer shell can take part in bonding. Silicon has four electrons available (there are another 8 and 2 in inner shells). These outer electrons are called valence electrons. When two atoms share each other's electrons, they form a bond, called a covalent bond (1-3). This bond joins the atoms together in a molecule. Molecules can either be unconnected to other molecules, like the oxygen molecule O_2, or can be linked together. Every silicon atom needs four oxygen atoms to form a molecule. Rather than forming single molecules, the silica molecules join together to form a giant network structure in which each silicon atom is joined to four oxygen atoms in a tetrahedron. Because each oxygen atom is shared by two silicon atoms (1-4), the overall formula is SiO_2.

In other compounds, such as sodium oxide, there is a different type of bonding called ionic bonding. The sodium atom gives up the single, negatively-charged electron in its outer shell to make a sodium ion with a single positive

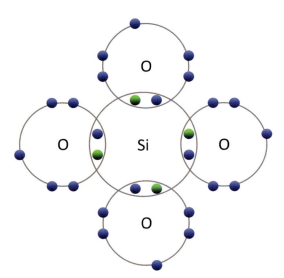

1-3. Covalent bonding between silicon and oxygen, which share electrons. The green electrons belong to the silicon atom.

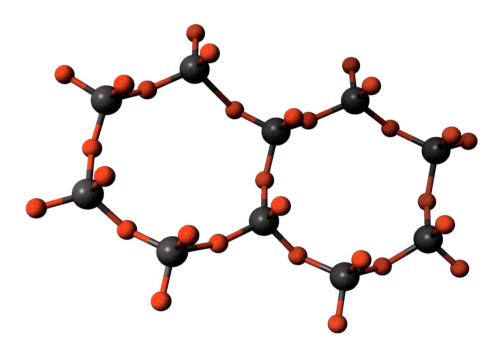

1-4. Diagram of network structure in silica. Each oxygen atom is joined to two silicon atoms. *Image: Elin Barrett.*

electrical charge. The electron fills a gap in the outer shell of the oxygen atom, which has six outer electrons. To complete the shell, the oxygen atom needs eight electrons, so it bonds with two sodium ions, each of which gives an electron to the oxygen outer shell (1-5). In general, metals form ionic bonds with non-metals, while non-metals form covalent bonds with other non-metals. However, most chemical bonds are partly ionic and partly covalent. The way in which atoms bond is determined by valency (number of electrons in the outer shell) and ionic radius. The sodium oxide compound has the formula Na_2O, where two sodium atoms are bonded to every oxygen atom. When this reacts with water, it becomes a strong alkali, sodium hydroxide, $NaOH$. For this reason, sodium and the similar metals lithium and potassium are called alkali metals. When sodium oxide reacts with silica, it breaks up the silica network structure, acting as a flux to melt the silica.

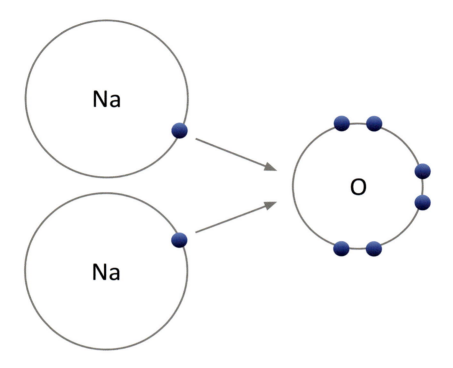

1-5. Ionic bonding between sodium and oxygen. The oxygen atom needs two extra electrons to complete its outer shell, so it takes one electron from each sodium atom.

Crystal Structure:
Cubic, Hexagonal, Close Packed, Spinel, Zircon

A crystal is a regular arrangement of atoms or molecules bonded together in a large structure. Many silicates, glaze materials and clays are made of crystals. As crystals are not only useful to potters but also a fascinating subject, we will explore the nature of crystals in some detail, in order to understand the behavior of these materials. Some, like quartz, have three-dimensional network structures, while others, such as clay, have layered sheet structures. Quartz crystals form when magma cools slowly and the atoms have time to arrange themselves in ordered layers, like stacked snooker balls. The crystal structure has an inherent symmetry, which is scaled up as the crystals grow larger, until they are visible to the naked eye. Quartz and feldspar crystals can grow up to several centimeters or more. Each type of crystal has its own particular symmetry, so for example, quartz crystals have hexagonal symmetry. They are a beautiful example of the arrangement of atoms, far too small to comprehend (an atom of silicon is so small that four million of them next to one another would only stretch to about a millimeter*), while affecting the shape of the quartz crystal you can hold in your hand. The crystal symmetry determines many of the crystal's properties, such as its shape, cleavage planes, and hardness. A crystal where the atoms are arranged at the corners of a cube (such as rock salt) will cleave or break differently from one where the atoms are arranged in a structure where the angles between cleavage planes are not 90° (such as calcite or dolomite).

There are a number of ways of lining up the atoms in a crystal. The arrangement of the atoms in the crystal lattice is governed by the way the atoms bond together. The structural arrangement will affect the properties such as the shape, and even the color of the crystal. A unit cell is the smallest unit which can be repeated to build a crystal lattice. The simplest unit cell is a cube (1-6), in which there are atoms at each of the eight corners. If there is an atom at the center of the cube, it is known as the body-centered cubic lattice structure. A similar crystal lattice is the face-centered cubic structure, which has atoms at the centers of each of the cube's six faces as well as at the corners. Crystals which have the face-centered cubic lattice structure include diamond, silicon, and spinel. This is a very stable structure, also known as a close-packed structure as it has the densest possible packing of atoms. As a result the minerals with this structure, such as diamond, are very hard. Some ceramic stains have the spinel structure, which is also very stable when fired in a glaze. In diamond, all the atoms are the same type (carbon), while in spinel, there are three different types of atom; magnesium, aluminium, and oxygen.

It is useful to learn about how the atoms are lined up in other minerals in order to identify them and better understand their properties, such as their cleavage and hardness. The next three unit cells still have right angles but not all the faces are square. The tetragonal crystal unit cell is similar to cubic except that all but two of its faces are rectangular rather than square (1-7). Zirconium silicate (zircon) and rutile have tetragonal crystals, which often form elongated needles. The orthorhombic crystal unit cell is like the cubic but with all of its faces rectangular instead of square. Mullite, witherite (barium carbonate) and celestine (strontium sulphate) have orthorhombic crystals. In stoneware and porcelain, mullite crystals grow at the glaze-clay body interface and form a strong, interlocking glaze-body layer.

*A note about units. 1 meter=1000 millimeters (mm) =1,000,000 micrometers (μm) =1,000,000,000 nanometers (nm). Light wavelength is around 500nm. Atom spacing is around 0.5nm.

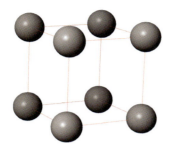

1-6. Simple cubic unit cell.

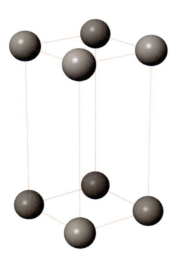

1-7. Tetragonal unit cell. Rutile has this structure and grows long, needle-shaped crystals.

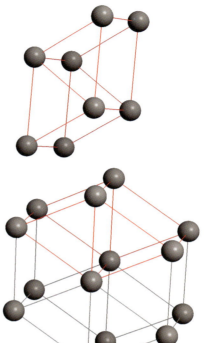

1-8. Hexagonal unit cell. Tridymite, high-temperature silica, has this crystal lattice structure.

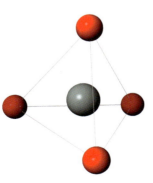

1-9. Diagram of silica tetrahedron. The gray atom is silicon, the red atoms are oxygen.

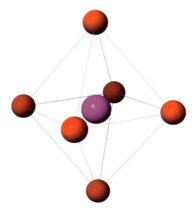

1-10. Alumina octahedron with six oxygen atoms arranged around an aluminium atom.
Images 1-6–1-10: Elin Barrett.

The monoclinic crystal lattice is similar to this, except two of the faces are parallelograms rather than rectangles. Minerals with this structure include orthoclase (potash feldspar) and petalite (lithium feldspar). Orthoclase comes from the Greek word "right fracture," meaning the two cleavage planes of this feldspar are at right angles. This helps geologists (and potters) to identify the various types of feldspar. The triclinic lattice structure is one in which none of the faces are at right angles, and is the least symmetrical of all unit cells. Minerals with a triclinic crystal structure include kaolinite (clay), albite (soda feldspar), microcline (another form of potash feldspar), and plagioclase (soda-calcia feldspar), from the Greek word "oblique fracture." Kaolin crystals appear almost hexagonal (see chapter 3), but are not perfect hexagons, owing to the underlying triclinic lack of symmetry.

Other crystal lattice structures are based on hexagonal symmetry (1-8). One of these is the rhombohedral unit cell, which is like a cube but with rhombus or diamond-shaped faces. Dolomite and calcite have this lattice structure. Haematite (red iron oxide, Fe_2O_3) also has this structure, although magnetite, Fe_3O_4 is cubic. Quartz and corundum (alumina) have the trigonal crystal system, which is also based on a hexagon, but with threefold symmetry. Quartz is composed of tetrahedra (1-9), with each silicon atom surrounded by four oxygen atoms. The tetrahedra are arranged in a hexagonal pattern but each pyramid is orientated in a different direction, which means they do not have sixfold symmetry. Quartz is actually made of chains composed of a repeating helix of three silica tetrahedra. An ideal quartz crystal is a six-sided prism* ending in a six-sided pyramid (1-11). The high-temperature version of quartz, tridymite, has the hexagonal structure. Alumina has trigonal (threefold) crystal symmetry but each aluminium atom is surrounded by six oxygen atoms arranged in an octahedron (1-10). Alumina has an almost hexagonal close-packed structure, making the material very hard. In all, there are seven lattice systems, which describe all crystal structures (1-12).

1-11. Quartz crystal, 1¾ inches long.

Lattice System	Symmetry/Geometry	Mineral	Hardness
Triclinic	No symmetry	Kaolinite (china clay)	2
Monoclinic	Parallelogram-based prism*	Orthoclase (potash feldspar)	6
Orthorhombic	Rectangle-based prism*	Witherite (barium carbonate)	3
Rhombohedral	Rhombus-faced cube	Dolomite	4
Tetragonal	Square-based prism*	Zircon	7½
Hexagonal	Hexagonal/Trigonal	Quartz	7
Cubic	Body-centered/Face-centered	Spinel	8

1-12. The seven crystal lattice systems, from the least to most symmetric. Mineral examples are given, as well as the hardness of each mineral listed.

*Geometric shapes: A prism is a flat-ended solid object with the same cross-section along its length. Glass prisms used to disperse colors in light often have a triangular cross-section. However, crystals in nature are often based on square, rectangular or hexagonal-based prisms. A rhombus is a parallelogram with sides of equal length, like the diamond suit in playing cards (1-13 and 1-14).

A large variety of different crystal structures can be made using the seven basic crystal lattices. This is because crystal lattices can have extra atoms as well as the ones at the corners or centered in the faces of the unit cell. These are usually smaller than the corner atoms and are known as interstitial atoms. If the interstitial atoms are

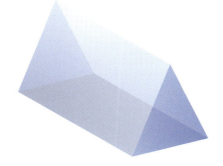 

1-13. Prism. A prism is a flat-ended solid object with the same cross-section along its length.

1-14. Rhombus. A rhombus is a parallelogram with four sides of equal length.

surrounded by four other atoms (like Si in silica), they are called tetrahedral interstices. If they are surrounded by six atoms arranged in an octahedron (like Al in alumina), they are called octahedral interstices. The position of interstitial transition metal atoms in the lattice can affect the color of the crystal. If the transition metal atom is in the octahedral position, the color will be different from the same metal atom in a tetrahedral position.

In spinel $MgAl_2O_4$, there are both tetrahedral and octahedral interstices (1-15). The oxygen atoms form a face-centered cubic unit cell, with magnesium atoms in tetrahedral interstitial positions and aluminium atoms in octahedral positions. As well as interstitial atoms, there can also be substitutions, where an atom in the crystal lattice is replaced by a different atom. If some magnesium and aluminium atoms are substituted by transition metals, for example, iron and chromium, the spinel will be colored and can be used as a stain for clay bodies and glazes. Iron and cobalt can replace the magnesium atoms, while chromium replaces the aluminium atoms. Iron chromite is brown, while cobalt chromite is blue-green, and cobalt iron chromite is black. Magnetite, Fe_3O_4 has the same spinel structure, with some iron (Fe) atoms in tetrahedral sites and some in octahedral sites. Magnetite (also known by potters as iron spangles) is a hard mineral, which is difficult to grind. It can be used to add speckle to clay bodies.

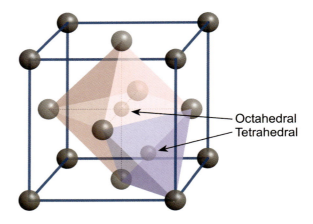

1-15. In the face-centered cubic unit cell, there is room for smaller, interstitial atoms in octahedral or tetrahedral positions.

Substitutions also occur in feldspar and clay. In clay, some of the silicon atoms are often substituted by aluminium, which can be substituted in turn by magnesium and iron. This affects the color of the clay as well as its firing properties (see chapter 3 on clay).

Mohs' Scale of Hardness

This scale of mineral hardness is not only useful when identifying minerals and rocks, it can also help with formulating scratch resistant glass and glazes. Glass has a hardness of 6, while knife blades have a hardness of around 5½. It can be seen from the list to the right that magnesium and calcium minerals tend to be relatively soft, while silica and alumina are much harder. Some minerals such as kyanite $Al_2O_3 \cdot SiO_2$ form elongated crystals, which have a hardness of 5 along the grain and 7 perpendicular to it. Minerals with giant covalent network structures such as quartz and feldspar are generally hard. However, hardness also depends on the size and shape of the crystals. Kaolinite has very small plate-like crystals which form a soft mass easily scraped by a fingernail.

Color in Glazes

Why are some materials transparent and others opaque? Light can be thought of as a beam of light particles called photons, each one a packet of light energy. When a photon of light hits an atom, it can be absorbed by electrons, which can jump to higher energy levels. This only happens if the light has the right amount of energy required for the electron to jump to a higher level. Light in the form of photons

Mohs' Scale of Hardness
1. Talc (magnesium silicate)
2. Gypsum (calcium sulphate)
3. Calcite (calcium carbonate)
4. Fluorite (calcium fluoride)
5. Apatite (calcium phosphate)
6. Orthoclase (potash feldspar)
7. Quartz (silica)
8. Topaz (alumino-silicate with fluorine)
9. Corundum (alumina)
10. Diamond (carbon)

Potter's Materials Hardness
1. Talc (magnesium silicate)
2. Kaolinite (china clay)
3. Calcite (calcium carbonate)
3½. Strontianite (strontium carbonate)
4. Dolomite (calcium magnesium carbonate)
4½. Colemanite (calcium borate)
5. Wollastonite (calcium silicate)
6. Albite (soda feldspar)
6½. Rutile (titanium dioxide)
7. Quartz (silica)
7½. Zirconium silicate
8. Spinel (magnesium aluminate)
9. Corundum (alumina)
9½. Silicon carbide

will have a frequency which our eyes interpret as color. The amount of energy of a photon depends on the particular frequency of the light, or its color. In glass, visible light does not have sufficient energy to move the electrons up to the next level, so instead it passes straight through and the glass looks transparent. Light with higher frequency such as ultraviolet light, does have enough energy, which is why UV light does not pass through glass. In this case, the glass absorbs the energy from the UV light and becomes warmer. The atoms in the glass become excited and vibrate, which can be felt as heat.

Why are things different colors? The origin of color can be understood by investigating what happens at the atomic level. Atoms are not colored in themselves. Carbon in graphite (pencil lead) is metallic gray and in its other well-known form, diamond is transparent and colorless. The colors we see all around us are the effects of light hitting objects and being partially absorbed. The remaining light that is not absorbed is reflected into our eyes. When the same objects are viewed in different colored light, they appear to be different colors. Transparent, colorless materials absorb no light, while black objects absorb all the light. Because color only exists in the reflected light from an object or in the light that passes through a transparent object it is accurate to say that when it is dark and an object has no light hitting it, then it has no color. Light is a form of energy, the visible part of the electromagnetic spectrum between ultraviolet and infrared (1-16). Invisible parts of the spectrum are x-rays, microwaves, and radio waves.

The structure, composition, and impurities in a crystal affect the material's interaction with light and hence its color. Colors in gemstones such as sapphire and

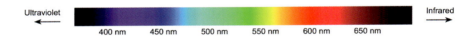

1-16. The color spectrum of visible light showing the wavelength in nanometers (a nanometer is a millionth of a millimeter). A shorter wavelength means higher energy.

ruby are caused by trace amounts of transition metal elements. Both these minerals are crystalline alumina, also known as corundum. In ruby, trace amounts of chromium produce a red color, while in sapphire, iron, and titanium cause a blue color. The red color in ruby comes from the way the electron cloud around the chromium atom is affected by the surrounding oxygen atoms in the alumina crystal, which is explained later in this chapter. However, in the case of sapphire, the blue color comes from transfer of electrons between the iron and titanium ions when light shines on the crystal. (An ion is an atom or molecule that has lost or gained an electron.)

Glazes can also be colored by adding transition metal oxides. The transition metal elements have an inner orbital which is only partially filled, allowing electrons to move between the different energy levels, in the same way that a solitaire board has an empty hole to allow the player to move the marbles around. When these elements form oxides or silicates in a glass, the energy levels of their electrons split into two groups (1-24). The energy gap corresponds exactly to the wavelength of a certain color of light, particularly (in glazes) yellow, orange or red light. When light passes through a colored glaze, electrons are able to move from the lower energy level to the higher one by absorbing a specific wavelength of light. The remaining light is the color we see. For example, cobalt silicate in glazes absorbs yellow light, so the reflected light we see is the complementary color, blue. Transition metals are able to bond with oxygen in either six-fold (octahedral) or four-fold (tetrahedral) co-ordination (1-18 and 1-19). Blue cobalt silicate has four-fold co-ordination while pink cobalt silicate (1-20) occurs in pyroxene crystals, which have a higher ratio of oxygen to silicon, with six-fold co-ordination (see chapter 2 for more on pyroxene). The color of light absorbed is affected by the shape of the electron cloud around the metal atom (1-17) and hence the splitting of the energy levels. In glazes, the fluxes present will also influence the shape of the electron cloud. For example, copper oxide in a glaze fired in oxidation

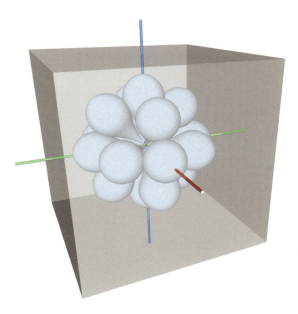

1-17. Transition metals have unfilled inner orbitals, called d orbitals. Up to two electrons are located in each orbital. There are 5 d orbitals, each orientated in a different direction. When they are superimposed, the electron cloud looks like a blackberry.

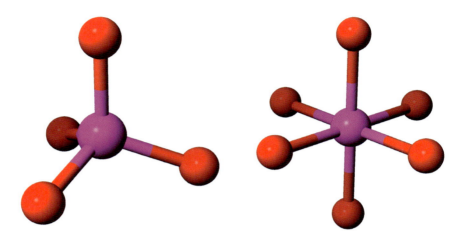

1-18. Tetrahedral arrangement, with metal atom e.g. cobalt in the center. The red atoms are oxygen. This arrangement with cobalt gives a blue color in glazes.

1-19. Octahedral arrangement, with metal atom e.g. cobalt in the center. The red atoms are oxygen. This arrangement with cobalt gives a pink color in glazes. Chromium and iron are more commonly found in this arrangement. *Images 1-18 and 1-19: Elin Barrett.*

1-20. Linda Bloomfield's small porcelain bowls, left cobalt blue magnesium matte, right, cobalt pink magnesium matte glaze.

absorbs red light, so the color we see is green. If the glaze is high in sodium and low in alumina, the electron cloud becomes distorted, the energy gap becomes wider, orange light (with higher energy than red light) is absorbed and the color we see is turquoise. The transition metal oxides tend to give blues, greens, and brown colors in glazes (1-21 and 1-22). The glaze color depends on the transition metal, the predominant fluxes in the glaze and whether it is fired in oxidation or reduction. Red, orange, and

1-21 Linda Bloomfield's thrown porcelain tableware, diameter 10 in. (26 cm), copper turquoise, praseodymium yellow, and cobalt-nickel gray glazes. *Image: Emma Lee*.

1-22. Tanya Gomez' *The Deluge*, thrown porcelain with blue glazes fired in reduction, to 12 in. (30 cm), 2010.

yellow are more difficult to produce (in either oxidation or reduction), often requiring industrially produced stains made from cadmium and selenium.

Stains

Stains are made by calcining (heating) together coloring oxides, silica, and some alumina in a kiln. They are ground into a powder which can be mixed into a glaze or used as an underglaze color. The particles of colored stain do not dissolve in the glaze like coloring oxides, but remain suspended as small particles. As they have already been fired, the color does not change on firing in a glaze. As well as spinels (mentioned earlier in this chapter), stains can be made by heating vanadium oxide with zirconium silicate. The vanadium is substituted for some of the zirconium and gives a range of blue-green colors. Yellow and red stains are made using cadmium and selenium. The stain particles can be stabilized by including them in a matrix of zirconium silicate. These are known as inclusion pigments or encapsulated stains. Other types of stains such as chrome-tin pink are stabilized using tin oxide. As a result, stains cause glazes to become opaque, while coloring oxides will dissolve to give transparent colored glazes. The solubility of coloring oxides increases with firing temperature and the presence of fluxes such as sodium, lithium, barium, and boron.

The Chemistry of Color

We have touched on the influence on color of the shape of the electron cloud around transition metal atoms. Here is a more detailed explanation of why transition metal ions are colored. This is quite complex chemistry but also very interesting and begins to reveal how colors emerge from the ingredients that make up a glaze.

Orbitals

At the beginning of this chapter, the structure of the atom was described as having electrons arranged in orbitals like planets in the solar system. The orbitals are actually much more complicated. Each shell of electrons contains sub-orbitals, each of which can hold two electrons, which, rather than following a path like a planet, can be anywhere within the orbital. Unlike planets, the electrons can act like both particles and waves and can vibrate. The first orbitals to fill with electrons are spherical and are named s orbitals. The alkali metals and alkaline earths only have s orbitals in their outermost shell and are called "s block" elements. The second set of orbitals to fill are shaped like a figure of eight and are called p orbitals. Electrons can be anywhere

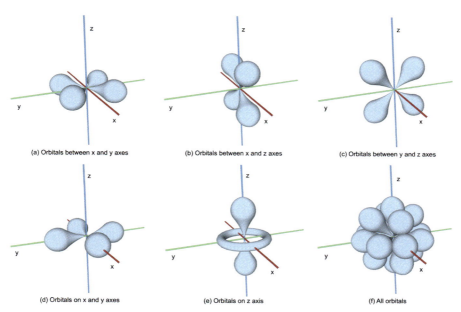

1-23. Transition metals have unfilled inner orbitals, called d orbitals. Up to two electrons are located in each orbital. There are 5 d orbitals, each orientated in a different direction. When they are superimposed, the electron cloud looks like a blackberry.

within in the two lobes of the p orbital. There are three p orbitals, each orientated in a different direction around the nucleus. The third set of orbitals are called d orbitals. These each have four lobes and there are five of them, each arranged in a different orientation, including a strange ring-shaped one (1-23). The transition metals have d orbitals in their third shell and are known as d-block elements. In transition metals, the s orbitals in the fourth shell start to fill before the d orbitals in the third shell, leaving some of the inner orbitals empty. This is what allows the electron transitions which give rise to color. The rare earth elements at the bottom of the periodic table also have seven f orbitals, which have even more complicated shapes. When all the orbitals are superimposed, the atom looks like a blackberry, with multiple lobes where the electrons are located. Only elements or ions with incomplete d or f orbitals can form colored compounds. The shapes of the d orbitals are important in explaining how some minerals, gemstones, and glazes appear colored.

Crystal Field Theory

This theory explains the color of complex compounds, where there is a central transition metal atom surrounded by electron rich atoms or molecules. These are called coordination complexes and commonly have six-fold or four-fold symmetry. In a crystal such as ruby, which has chromium substituted for some of the aluminium atoms, the surrounding atoms are oxygen atoms fixed in the crystal lattice structure. In a glaze, the surrounding molecules are silica, as well as sodium, potassium, and calcium ions. The molecules are linked but disordered and are free to move around in the molten glaze.

In a molten glaze, when silicate ions move near a transition metal atom, they are repelled more along certain directions. In an octahedral complex, where six ions approach, one from the center of each face of a cube, the highest repulsion is from the orbitals aligned along the x, y, and z axes (1-24). As the ions approach, the energy level of these orbitals is raised i.e. electrons need more energy to move there. The lowest repulsion is from the orbitals aligned between the axes. The energy of these orbitals is lowered. The energy level split between the two sets of orbitals happens to be the same

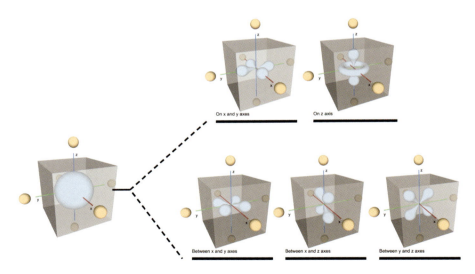

1-24. On the left is a metal atom with six negative ions around it. When six ions approach in order to bond with the central atom, the ions approaching along the axes are repelled more by the electrons in d orbitals aligned along the axes. Those d orbitals are therefore raised to a higher energy level i.e. electrons need more energy to move there. The electrons in the d orbitals lying between the axes repel the approaching ions less strongly. The energy level of those d orbitals is lowered. Color results from electron transitions between the lower- and higher-energy d orbitals. The energy levels are shown as horizontal black lines. The x, y, and z axes are red, green, and blue lines.

as the energy of some visible light. When light hits the metal atom, a specific color is absorbed and the electrons move from the lower energy orbitals to the higher ones. The color we see is the remaining light reflected from the metal atom. In glazes, the energy level splitting is relatively small, so the colors absorbed are at the low energy end of the spectrum (red, orange, yellow), and the colors we see are greens and blues. In ruby, the oxygen atoms are fixed in a crystal lattice and are forced closer to the chromium atoms, giving a larger energy level splitting. The chromium in ruby absorbs the higher energy green light and the reflected light we see is red.

Chromium and iron are often found in six-fold, octahedral coordination. Four-fold, tetrahedral coordination is more common in cobalt complexes. In tetrahedral complexes, the four ions approach the central atom from alternate corners of a cube and do not meet much repulsion as the orbitals are not aligned in opposing directions. The energy level splitting is smaller but the asymmetric shape of the complex means that more orbitals are available for electrons to move into and this is the reason cobalt is such a strong colorant in glazes.

When coloring oxides are fired in a glaze, they react with the silica to become silicates and the electron cloud around each coloring metal atom changes from the arrangement in an oxide to a different arrangement in a silicate. This is why coloring oxides usually change color on firing. Once the glaze has cooled and solidified with a particular arrangement of atoms, the color is locked into the glaze.

The Potter's Periodic Table

The periodic table (1-25) explains the chemical and physical properties of the different materials used by potters. It is the basis for understanding the whole of chemistry. However, we are primarily interested in the elements useful to potters, which include silicon, aluminium, the alkali metals and alkaline earths, as well as the transition metals.

During the nineteenth century, scientists began to notice that groups of elements had similar properties. Not all the elements had yet been discovered, but when they were lined up in order of increasing atomic number in seven rows, similarities between groups became clear. We know now that is because the elements in a group all have the same number of electrons in their outer shell, so they all react in similar ways.

In the periodic table, the elements are listed in order of ascending atomic number. There are 7 rows of elements and 18 columns. The elements in each column, called a group, have similar properties. Important groups for the potter are group 1, the alkali metals (sodium, potassium etc.), and group 2, the alkaline earths (calcium, magnesium

Science for Potters

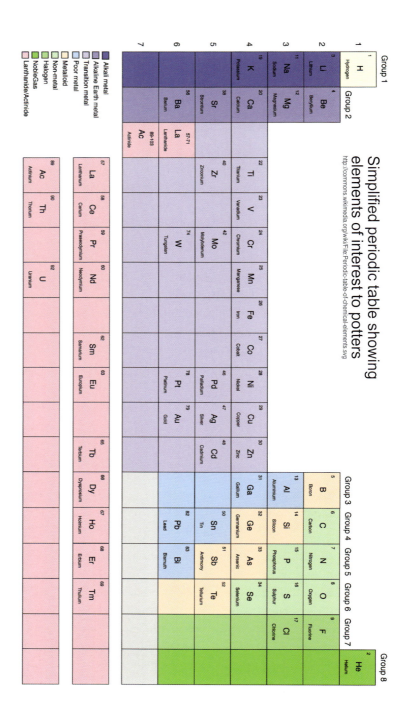

1-25. The potter's periodic table. Elements useful to potters. The gaps in the table are elements not used in ceramics. Some elements are only present in ceramics in trace amounts, but are included for completeness, e.g. Germanium, Arsenic.

etc.) These are used as fluxes in glazes. All the elements on the left-hand side and middle of the periodic table are metals. The ones at the bottom are known as heavy metals as they have more protons and neutrons and therefore greater atomic weights.

The central block of the periodic table contains the transition metals. These can have several oxidation states and are important in producing colored glazes, particularly the metals along the top row: chromium, manganese, iron, cobalt, nickel, and copper. The two rows inserted at the bottom are known as the lanthanides and the actinides, and some can also produce colors in glass and glazes. Uranium is the heaviest naturally occurring element and can produce yellow in glazes (used by studio potter Lucie Rie on her bowls) although it is no longer used owing to its radioactivity. The elements beyond uranium can only be synthesized in particle accelerators and decay radioactively into other elements. Lead is the heaviest stable, non-radioactive element.

On the right-hand side of the periodic table is a diagonal line, which divides metals from non-metals. The elements on this line include boron, silicon, and arsenic. They are known as metalloids and are semiconductors, which means they will only conduct electricity under certain conditions. Silicon in the form of single crystal wafers is the basis of modern electronics and computers. Some of the elements most useful to potters also lie on or near this dividing line and include silicon and boron, both glass formers although the latter is mainly used as a flux in low-temperature glazes and in heat-resistant borosilicate glass (Pyrex). Aluminium is next to silicon, found in clay and used as a stabilizer in glazes, preventing them from becoming too runny when fired. On the right-hand side of silicon is phosphorus, used as a flux in glazes and in bone china. Antimony and selenium are used in small amounts as yellow and red colorants in glazes.

The top right hand corner of the periodic table contains oxygen, the halogens fluorine and chlorine, and the noble gases helium and neon. Oxygen is present in all clay and glazes, usually combined with silicon and aluminium as oxides. Fluorine is of interest to the potter, as it is often given off in the kiln from decomposing fluorspar, a mineral found in Cornwall Stone from the UK.

Metals and Non-Metals

Most of the elements in the periodic table are metals. Many of the metals discovered since the early nineteenth century have names ending in "-ium," for example, sodium, calcium, barium. Their oxides form alkaline solutions when dissolved in water. The oxides, rather than the metals, are of most interest to the potter as they are the constituents of clay and glazes. The non-metals include carbon and phosphorus, which form acidic oxides, which means that their oxides dissolve in water to make acidic solutions. Carbon is found in glaze materials such as sodium carbonate, which breaks down during firing and gives off carbon dioxide. This escapes from the kiln as a gas, so the carbon does not remain in the fired glaze (except in a type of glaze known as carbon trap). Carbon in organic matter present in clay will also form carbon dioxide when fired and escape from the kiln. Between the metals and non-metals is a group known as the metalloids or semiconductors, which includes boron and silicon. These are very useful to potters as they are the glass formers, used to make glazes and to vitrify the clay body.

Trends Across a Period
Moving from left to right on the periodic table, an extra electron is added to the outer shell of each atom. The valence therefore increases so that each successive element will combine with more oxygen. For example, the oxides in the third row from the top are Na_2O, MgO, Al_2O_3, SiO_2, P_2O_5. Oxygen has six electrons in its outer shell so needs two more electrons to complete the shell. Sodium has a valence of 1 and so two sodium atoms are needed for every oxygen atom. Magnesium has a valence of 2 and combines with one oxygen atom. Aluminium has a valence of three, silicon four, and phosphorus five, so the number of oxygen atoms increases to five oxygen for every two phosphorus atoms.

The far left of the periodic table is highly alkaline and the right is highly acidic. The strength of the alkali decreases from left to right, while the strength of the acid increases. For example, along the third row, sodium oxide Na_2O is highly alkaline, magnesium oxide MgO is alkaline, aluminium oxide Al_2O_3 is amphoteric (it can act either as an acid or base), silicon dioxide SiO_2 is acidic and phosphorus pentoxide P_2O_5 is highly acidic. In ceramic glazes and vitreous clay bodies, the alkaline and acidic oxides react together and melt. The alkaline metal oxides are fluxes, which react with the acidic glass former, silica. The elements in the central block are amphoteric, although many show slightly alkaline or acidic properties. Their oxides are used in glazes as supplementary fluxes, stabilizers, opacifiers, and colorants. Moving along the period in the central block, electrons are added to an incomplete inner shell.

Across the periodic table, the elements are metals on the left and center and non-metals on the top right. The metallic character (the ability to donate electrons and form an alkali/base) decreases from left to right and increases from top to bottom. The atom size also decreases from left to right. As extra protons are added to the nucleus, the electrons are attracted more strongly and pulled in closer to the nucleus.

Trends Down a Group

The atom size and weight increases down a group. The lightest elements are at the top of the periodic table, the heaviest at the bottom. Going down a group, electrons are added to outer shells, and are shielded from the nucleus by the electrons in the inner shells. The melting points of elements and their oxides tend to decrease down the group as the larger-sized atoms will more readily give up their electrons in chemical reactions (1-36).

Metals
Group 1: The Alkali Metals

Group 1 (1-26) includes lithium (Li), sodium (Na), and potassium (K). They are extremely reactive metals and react vigorously with water, sometimes bursting into flames. They are not found naturally in their metallic state but only in combination with other elements. Their oxides are strong fluxes and help to melt the silica in a glaze. Their fluxing ability decreases down the group. The alkali metal oxides are found in feldspars and they are also available in the more soluble carbonate form. The oxides have the chemical formula R_2O, where R is the metal and O is oxygen.

Lithium is the least reactive of the alkali metals but its oxide has the highest fluxing power in glazes. Lithium oxide melts at a higher temperature than sodium and potassium but once melted, forms a more fluid melt. Lithium has a small atom size and is the lightest metal, so compared to sodium, weight for weight, only a small amount is needed to flux a glaze. Lithium oxide has a lower expansion rate than the other alkali metals and is used in shock-resistant, heatproof ovenware. It also increases the hardness of glazes.

Sodium oxide is a stronger flux than potassium oxide. It has a higher melting point than potassium oxide but produces a more fluid melt. However, it is volatile above 2327°F (1275°C) and can cause the glaze to bubble. It has a high expansion rate and can cause crazing in glazes.

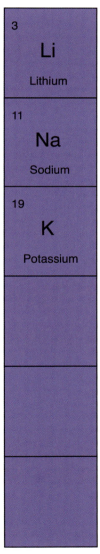

1-26. Group 1, the alkali metals used in ceramics.

Potassium oxide begins to melt at a slightly lower temperature but has a wider firing range than sodium oxide, so can be used at higher firing temperatures. It produces a more viscous glaze, which is harder and more resistant to scratching than a sodium-based glaze.

Group 2: The Alkaline Earths

Group 2 (1-27) of the periodic table includes magnesium (Mg), calcium (Ca), strontium (Sr), and barium (Ba). They are reactive metals but not as reactive as the alkali metals in group 1. The oxides of the alkaline earth metals are used as secondary fluxes in glazes. They have surprisingly high melting temperatures, but act in eutectic mixtures to lower the melting point of the glaze (1-37). (A eutectic is the lowest melting combination of two materials.) They also stabilize the glaze and make it more durable. The oxides have the chemical formula RO, where R is the metal and O is oxygen. The oxides and carbonates are not soluble in water.

Calcium oxide is the most widely available alkaline earth oxide. It is used to make matte glazes and as a flux at firing temperatures above 2012°F (1100°C).

Magnesium oxide is used to make satin matte glazes and has a low expansion rate, useful for correcting crazing. It has a higher melting point than calcium oxide and is an active flux above 2138°F (1170°C).

Barium oxide can be used as a flux above 2147°F (1175°C) and to make matte glazes. However, its source material, barium carbonate is toxic. Strontium oxide can be used as an alternative, non-toxic flux above 1994°F (1090°C). It has properties similar to calcium and sits between calcium and barium in the group. Barium and strontium mattes give brighter colors than magnesium and calcium, which tend to bleach out colors. Barium and strontium can be used at earthenware temperatures, particularly if they have first been made into a frit.

1-27. Group 2, the alkaline earths.

The lightest member of this group is beryllium, found in the mineral beryl, in gemstones emerald and aquamarine. Although its oxide acts as a flux, it is not used by potters as it is expensive and very toxic.

The Transition Metals

Acidic

TiO$_2$	V$_2$O$_3$		MnO	FeO	CoO	NiO	Cu$_2$O
	V$_2$O$_5$	Cr$_2$O$_3$	MnO$_2$	Fe$_2$O$_3$			CuO

Alkaline

1-28. Transition metal coloring oxides. Those with with acidic tendencies are shown in red and alkaline tendencies are shown in blue.

The transition metals (1-28 and 1-29) can each have several different oxidation states, meaning they can combine with different numbers of oxygen atoms, depending on the surrounding conditions. They have an incomplete inner shell of electrons, which allows the electrons to move around between energy levels. The transition metals (or rather, their oxides) most important to potters are called the coloring oxides. These are found on the top row of the transition metal block and are the smallest-sized transition metal atoms. They include titanium (Ti), vanadium (V), chromium (Cr), manganese (Mn), iron (Fe), cobalt (Co), nickel (Ni), and copper (Cu). Chromium oxide has the formula Cr$_2$O$_3$, and is amphoteric with acidic tendencies, while cobalt, nickel, and copper oxides have the formula RO and are amphoteric with alkaline tendencies. Manganese

22	23	24	25	26	27	28	29	30
Ti	V	Cr	Mn	Fe	Co	Ni	Cu	Zn
Titanium	Vanadium	Chromium	Manganese	Iron	Cobalt	Nickel	Copper	Zinc
40		42				46	47	48
Zr		Mo				Pd	Ag	Cd
Zirconium		Molybdenum				Palladium	Silver	Cadmium
		74				78	79	
		W				Pt	Au	
		Tungsten				Platinum	Gold	

1-29. Central block of the periodic table. Transition metals used in ceramics.

and iron oxide have several valencies, for example red (ferric) iron oxide Fe_2O_3 which is acidic and refractory and black (ferrous) iron oxide FeO which is basic/alkaline and acts as a flux. Copper oxide can give dramatically different colors in different conditions, including green in oxidation and ox-blood red in reduction.

Although it is in the same block, zinc (Zn) is not technically a transition metal as its inner shell is completely filled with electrons. Its oxide is used not as a colorant, but as a flux in mid-temperature glazes. In the next row of the periodic table, of interest to potters are zirconium (Zr), used to opacify glazes, and cadmium (Cd), used in yellow glaze stains. Molybdenum (Mo) and Tungsten (W) are used in iridescent crystalline glazes. Silver (Ag), copper (Cu), gold (Au), and platinum (Pt) can be used by potters in metallic lusters. Other transition metal elements niobium (Nb) and tantalum (Ta) have properties similar to zirconium and are used to increase the refractive index in glass lenses.

1-30. Lanthanides or rare earths used in ceramics.

The Rare Earths

The rare earth elements cerium (Ce), praseodymium (Pr), neodymium (Nd), holmium (Ho), and erbium (Er) are used to color glass and, in the case of praseodymium, to make a yellow stain for glazes. They were originally found mixed together and were difficult to separate as they have very similar chemical properties. Neodymium means "new twin" and is found mixed with praseodymium, meaning "green twin," from the Greek word "prasios didymos" and the pure oxides give respectively a violet and green color in glazes (1-31). The rare earths are also known as the lanthanides as they follow the element lanthanum in the periodic table. They are refractory and have the theoretical formulae CeO_2, PrO_2, Nd_2O_3, and Er_2O_3. They are weak colorants but can be used in glazes on porcelain. The insoluble oxides are not toxic, although the firing fumes should be avoided. Some of the other lanthanides (samarium, europium, terbium, dysprosium, and thulium) can give bright flourescent glaze colors, but only under ultraviolet light. Though not particularly rare, they are currently only mined in China and have recently become very expensive. They are extracted from the mineral

Chemistry

1-31. Clockwise from top: erbium, praseodymium, and neodymium glazes on porcelain.

1-32. Monazite sand. Radioactive rare-earth phosphate mineral (Ce, La, Pr, Nd, Th, Y) PO_4.

monazite (1-32), which contains thorium and is radioactive, and bastnäsite.

The bottom row of the periodic table, the actinide series, contains uranium (U), which was used briefly by the Homer Laughlin China Co. to glaze their bright red, yellow, and orange colored Fiesta® dinnerware in the mid-twentieth century, but is now unobtainable owing to its radioactivity.

Poor Metals
Aluminium (Al), Tin (Sn), Lead (Pb)

The post-transition metals are poor metals (1-33). Although they look silvery like metals, they are weak metals, with low mechanical strength. They are chemically

29

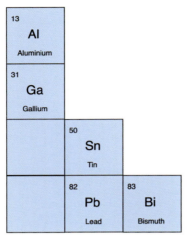

1-33. Post-transition metal triangle.

close to the non-metals and, being near the bottom of the periodic table, are relatively soft with low melting points.

Aluminium (Al) is the most abundant metal in the Earth's crust. It was named aluminium in the UK and later changed to aluminum in the US.

Aluminium oxide, or alumina, is found together with silica in clay, which is an aluminosilicate. Alumina is used to make glazes more viscous in the melt to prevent them running off the pot. Aluminium oxide has the formula Al_2O_3 and is amphoteric, capable of reacting with either alkali or acid. It has an extremely high melting point of 3722°F (2050°C). In its crystalline form, alumina forms a very hard mineral called corundum or sapphire, used to make scratch-resistant watch faces. It is the second hardest naturally occurring mineral after diamond.

Tin (Sn) is a metal also found in this group of elements. Tin oxide (SnO_2) is an acidic oxide used as an opacifier in glazes. It was originally used to cover coarse clay bodies with a white tin glaze, imitating the look of Chinese porcelain.

Lead oxide (PbO) was once used as the main flux in low temperature glazes but its use has now diminished owing to its toxicity and tendency to accumulate in the body. Lead bisilicate and sesquisilicate frits are still used in the UK and around the world, but have been superseded by borosilicate frits in the US.

Bismuth (Bi) is another metal found in this group, used by potters in mother-of-pearl lusters.

Semi-Metals

This diagonal group is known as the metalloids (1-34). They are generally hard and brittle and are semiconductors.

Boron (B) falls on the boundary between metals and non-metals. Its oxide can be used as a flux and, used together with sodium and calcium, it has replaced lead in earthenware glazes. Boric oxide is also a glass former and has a very low expansion rate. It is used to make heatproof borosilicate lab glass. Like all non-metals, it forms an acidic oxide, which has the chemical formula B_2O_3.

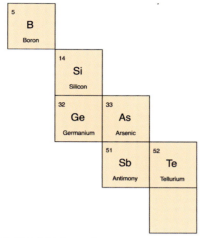

1-34. Metalloid diagonal.

Silicon (Si) is semiconductor and is a brittle, silvery-gray semi-metal used to make silicon chips in computers. Silicon dioxide (SiO_2), or silica, forms over 60% of the Earth's crust and is the basis of silicate minerals; rocks, sand, clays, and glazes. The name silicon comes from the Latin word "silex" meaning hard stone or flint. It was originally named "silicium," suggesting a metal, but the name was changed to "silicon," which sounds more like the non-metals carbon and boron. Some people confuse silicone rubber with silicon. The former is a type of synthetic organic polymer, containing silicon, oxygen, hydrogen, and carbon.

Silica melts to form a glass but has a high melting point of 3110°F (1710°C). However, if alumina is added in certain proportions, the resulting mixture will have a lower melting point than either of the pure constituents, known as a eutectic. Additional fluxes are required to melt it at the temperatures reached in a kiln. Silica is an acidic oxide, which reacts with alkaline metal fluxes.

Germanium, gallium, arsenic, and tellurium are present in trace amounts with other glaze colorants. They are used mainly in the semiconductor industry.

Antimony (Sb), a semi-metal, can be used in glazes, usually together with lead as a colorant found in low temperature yellow glazes. This was the bright yellow traditionally used on tin-glazed earthenware or majolica.

Non-Metals

The non-metals form acidic oxides (1-35). The acids become progressively stronger from left to right along the period, for example, phosphoric acid, sulphuric acid, hydrochloric acid. Hydrofluoric acid is very corrosive and can dissolve glass. When fluorine gas is given off from some clays during firing, it dissolves in water condensed on the windows and can etch the glass.

Carbon (C) is present as lignite (an intermediate between peat and coal) in fireclays and ball clays, and in carbonates used in glazes but it turns into carbon dioxide gas on heating and escapes from the kiln. Carbon dioxide dissolves in water to make a weak acid.

1-35. Non-metal triangle.

Phosphorus (P) is a non-metal and forms an acidic oxide. It is a glass former and is used with calcium in small quantities as a flux and opacifier in stoneware glazes, and in larger quantities in bone china. It is found in wood ash and bone ash (calcium phosphate).

Oxygen (O) is very reactive and is found in most glaze materials, either in the form of an oxide or carbonate, or combined with silicon in a silicate. It can combine with most other elements and is the most abundant element in the Earth's crust, as well as comprising over 20% of the Earth's atmosphere. All the chemical interactions in clay and glazes during firing involve oxides.

Sulphur (S) is sometimes present in clays and is given off during firing as sulphur dioxide. It is also present in some yellow glaze stains containing cadmium sulphide.

Selenium (Se) can also be used in glazes, usually together with cadmium as a colorant found in orange and red glaze stains.

From the periodic table, we can see that the alkaline metal oxides are important fluxes, which react during firing with the acidic glass-forming oxides in clays and glazes. We have seen how atoms combine together to make molecules, and how they can grow to form crystals. In the next chapter, we will look at how this process occurs naturally in the minerals and rocks formed in the Earth's crust, from which we take our clays and glaze materials.

Flux	Oxide Formula	Melting Point °F	Melting Point °C
Boron	B_2O_3	1292°	700°
Potassium	K_2O	1292°	700°
Lead	PbO	1616°	880°
Sodium	Na_2O	1652°°	900°
Lithium	Li_2O	3092°	1700°
Barium	BaO	3493°	1923°
Zinc	ZnO	3587°	1975°
Strontium	SrO	4406°	2430°
Calcium	CaO	4658°	2570°
Magnesium	MgO	5072°	2800°

Fig. 1-36. Melting points of fluxes The lower-melting oxides are used in earthenware glazes and the higher-temperature ones in stoneware glazes. However, in glazes they act in eutectic mixtures, which lower the melting point of both flux and silica. (*Information from* The Potter's Dictionary of Materials and Techniques, *by Frank and Janet Hamer, A & C Black, 1997.*)

Fluxing power (strongest at top)	Oxide Formula	Fluxing Action Begins at °F	Fluxing Action Begins at °C
Lithium	Li_2O	1472°	800°
Lead	PbO	1472°	800°
Boron	B_2O_3	1292°	700°
Sodium	Na_2O	1472°	800°
Potassium	K_2O	1382°	750°
Calcium	CaO	2012°	1100°
Strontium	SrO	1994°	1090°
Barium	BaO	2147°	1175°
Magnesium	MgO	2138°	1170°
Zinc	ZnO	1985°	1085°

Fig. 1-37. Fluxing power. This is the ability of the oxide to form a eutectic on melting. The more alkaline fluxes tend to have higher fluxing power. (*Information from* Glaze: The Ultimate Ceramic Artist's Guide to Glaze and Color, *by Brian Taylor and Kate Doody, Barron's, New York, 2014.*)

Kate Malone, *A Pair of Summer Rain Atomic Bottles*, 11 in. (28 cm) in length, crystalline glazed stoneware, 2014. *Image: Courtesy of Adrian Sassoon, London.*

Rhyolite Peak, Cumbria, UK. *Image: Matthew Blakely.*

CHAPTER 2

Geology for Potters

My father used to take me on rock hunting expeditions to Aust Cliff under the old Severn suspension bridge which joins England to Wales. The cliff has visible layers of red marl, tea green marl, and limestone. We found interesting rocks, fossils, and quartz crystals. When I started my first pottery studio and bought my first glaze materials I was living in California. I thought the names of the materials sounded very exotic, Custer feldspar from the Wild West and Edgar Plastic Kaolin (EPK) from Florida. Potters in Britain are more likely to use Cornish Stone and English China Clay, both found in Cornwall (see US/UK conversion table) (p. 65).

While writing this book, I researched geology, particularly the clays and rocks of England where I live, and the clays of eastern North America, where I was born. I have concentrated mainly on the geology of Great Britain and North America, which were once joined together and share similar features. However, materials similar to those covered in this chapter can be found worldwide and the natural processes which create and transform them are universal.

In this chapter, we will explore rocks, minerals and how they are formed from magma in the Earth's crust, and recycled through weathering and sedimentation. Many rocks are millions of years old, formed by the cooling of molten rock, either deep underground or at the surface in volcanic eruptions. The movement of tectonic plates causes the uplift of mountain ranges, which are gradually weathered by water, ice and wind. The weathered rock is deposited in layers and is eventually compressed and hardened into new rock. Many of these layers include clay, sand, and other glaze materials. When potters fire their clays and glazes in a kiln, they are enabling processes similar to those taking place when rocks are formed from molten magma. The temperature of magma ranges between 1292–2372°F (700–1300°C), the same temperature range as in a potter's kiln.

Rocks are composed of minerals, many of which are crystals with ordered atomic structures (see chapter 1). We will investigate the minerals used by potters, particularly those used in glazes such as feldspar, which comes from granite rock. The structure and properties of clay will be covered in more depth in chapter 3.

Clays and glazes are made of rocks and minerals from the Earth. Potters in the past used locally available materials such as locally dug clay and pulverized rocks, wood ash, and grass ash. This use of local materials led to many different names for clays and feldspars. Minerals used by the ceramic industry are now widely available to potters and it is useful to know their properties, as well as which materials can be substituted for others. Manufacturers will often make a synthetic version of a local material which is no longer mined. If we can understand the processes by which rocks and minerals were formed, it will help us to understand how clays and glazes melt during firing in the kiln.

> **Defining the Terms**
>
> **Felsic:** Light rock or mineral containing feldspar and silica.
>
> **Igneous:** Rocks formed from cooled magma.
>
> **Magma:** Molten rock.
>
> **Mafic:** Dark rock or mineral containing magnesium and iron.
>
> **Metamorphic:** Rocks formed from other rocks by pressure or heat.
>
> **Mineral:** An inorganic substance with an ordered atomic structure e.g. quartz.
>
> **Rock**: An aggregate of minerals, for example granite.
>
> **Sedimentary:** Rocks formed from deposited layers of sediment.

ROCKS

The most abundant elements in the Earth's crust are oxygen and silicon. Many rocks therefore contain silicate minerals, such as feldspar, which is an alumino-silicate (containing alumina and silica). Silicates can be divided into two types, the light and the dark silicates. The light-colored silicates include quartz and feldspar, which are the main constituents of granite and are used by the ceramic industry in both clays and glazes. The dark-colored silicates contain iron and magnesium and include minerals such as olivine and pyroxene. These make up the darker rocks such as fine-grained basalt and coarse-grained gabbro, which are sometimes used by potters, particularly those making glazes from locally sourced rocks. The alumino-silicates vary in structure according to how they are formed. Granite and basalt are both types of igneous rock, made by cooling and solidification of magma, either deep underground or from a volcanic eruption or lava flow. As the magma gradually cools, the solid igneous rock it forms changes in composition as a variety of minerals solidify from the melt, one after the other. In pottery, we often use the lighter colored, more easily melted rocks mined to produce the whiter ceramics favored by industry. In cooling magma, the magnesium, iron, and calcium crystallize out first, forming dark green-colored olivine (a group of minerals ranging from Fe_2SiO_4 to Mg_2SiO_4) and pyroxene (minerals ranging from $FeCaSi_2O_6$ to $MgCaSi_2O_6$). These ferro-magnesian silicates are heavier and have higher melting points than the lighter silicates in the magma, although once melted they are more fluid. The remaining liquid magma is high in sodium, potassium, and silica and this crystallizes as light-colored feldspar and quartz. This is lighter in weight, but more viscous, and often flows from large underground masses called plutons into cracks between other rocks, called sills (horizontal) and dykes (vertical). The light-colored silicates contain over 65% silica and are acidic. Intermediate rocks such as syenite and diorite can contain 55–65% silica. The dark-colored silicates contain only 45–55% silica and are therefore more alkaline. Silica is classified as an acidic oxide even though it is not readily soluble in water.

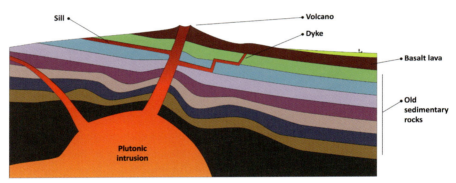

2-1. Diagram of volcano, plutonic intrusion, sills, and dykes.

The most unstable minerals, which break down and weather most easily, are the ones with the highest crystallization temperature. This is because they form single crystal structures rather than more stable frameworks. Olivine is the least stable and quartz is the most stable silicate mineral and therefore the least weathered. The dark silicates break down to the smallest particles, found in many clays such as bentonite, whereas quartz is often found in large crystals. The structure of silica (2-3) (and all silicates) is based on a tetrahedron (a triangle-based pyramid), with a silicon atom in the center and oxygen atoms at each of the four corners. In the dark (mafic) silicates such as olivine, each isolated silica tetrahedron is bonded with magnesium and iron, rather than with other silicon atoms. The magnesium and iron form ionic bonds,

Silicates	Order	Mineral	Formula	Structure
Dark (Mafic)	1	Olivine	FeMgSiO$_4$	Single tetrahedron
	2	Pyroxene	MgCaSi$_2$O$_6$	Single chain
	3	Amphibole		Double chain
	4	Biotite mica		Sheet
Light (Felsic)	1	Calcium feldspar	CaAl$_2$Si$_2$O$_8$	Framework
	2	Ca-Na plagioclase feldspar	NaAlSi$_3$O$_8$	Framework
	3	K orthoclase feldspar	KAlSi$_3$O$_8$	Framework
	4	Muscovite mica		Sheet
	5	Quartz	SiO$_2$	Framework

2-2. Amount of silica in each mineral. Bowen's reaction series. The order in which minerals solidify from magma. The amount of silica in each mineral increases from the dark to the light silicates.

which are less stable than the covalent bonds within the silica tetrahedra. Going from darker to lighter silicates, the silica tetrahedra are bonded in increasingly stable arrangements. In pyroxene, the silica tetrahedra are bonded together in chains, while in amphibole the chains join together to make double chains. In biotite and muscovite mica, the silica tetrahedra make up whole sheets. The underlying atomic structure is scaled up in the crystalline structure of mica, which forms pseudo-hexagonal plates visible to the eye. Mica breaks down to form illite clay, which has a similar sheet structure.

In feldspar (2-4) and quartz the silica tetrahedra are connected in three dimensions to form a framework structure, which is very stable. In feldspar, one in every four silicon atoms is replaced by aluminium and the larger spaces in the

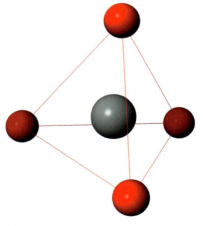

2-3. Silica tetrahedron, gray=silicon atom, red=oxygen atom.

structure are filled by sodium or potassium atoms. The difference in valence between the silicon and aluminium is compensated by the sodium or potassium.

Rocks can be classified into three types: igneous, metamorphic, and sedimentary. Igneous rocks are those which are formed from cooled magma. If the molten rock cools slowly deep beneath the earth's surface, the crystal size will be large and

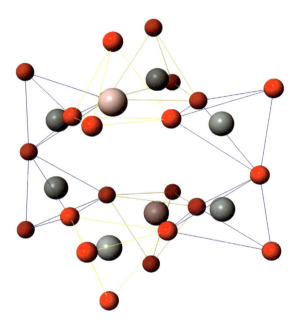

2-4. Feldspar structure, gray=silicon atom, red=oxygen atom, brown=aluminium atom. The sodium and potassium atoms are not shown but would be situated in the large spaces in between rings of silica tetrahedra. *Image: Elin Barrett.*

the granite coarse (2-5). This is known as plutonic or intrusive rock as it is often found in dykes intruding into other rocks. If the mineral crystals are very large (greater than 2 cm), the rock is called pegmatite and some types contain feldspars useful to potters. If magma cools quickly at the earth's surface, the crystals will be much smaller and the rock will have a finer grain size. This type of rock is known as volcanic or extrusive and includes light rhyolite (2-6) and dark basalt (2-7), formed from cooled lava (2-8 and 2-9). Rocks which are erupted by volcanoes can cool very fast and include frothy pumice, vesicular basalt, and glassy obsidian (2-10 and 2-11).

2-5. Granite from south Devon, England, 8 in. (20 cm) in length. The dark band and black crystals contain iron and magnesium. The glittery crystals are muscovite mica. The white and pink patches are feldspar and the gray areas are quartz. This is an intermediate type of granite known as granodiorite.

2-6. Rhyolite containing topaz crystals from Topaz Mountain, Utah.

2-7. Vesicular basalt from Sid Butte, Idaho, Snake River Plain, 18,000 years old.
Images 2-6 and 2-7: Matt Fiske.

The igneous rocks most useful to potters are felsic, yielding feldspars and silica, which are found together with mica in rock aggregates such as granite. Mica is a lustrous, sheet silicate mineral, which forms thin, flat, hexagonal crystals. There are several types of mica, including silvery muscovite, dark biotite, and purple lepidolite.

Metamorphic rocks are those that have been transformed by heat or pressure. For example, under pressure, shale becomes slate and limestone turns into marble. More extreme pressures can give rise to metamorphic rocks such as gneiss and schist, which

2-8. Line blend of rhyolite and basalt. Left rhyolite, 75:25, 50:50, 25:75, right basalt. The rocks were crushed, then ball milled, and fired to cone 12 (2286°F (1252°C)) in oxidation. The glaze with 75% rhyolite and 25% basalt is an oilspot glaze, where iron oxide has released oxygen during firing, which has bubbled through the glaze. *Image: Matt Fiske.*

	SiO$_2$	TiO$_2$	Al$_2$O$_3$	Fe2O3	Mn$_2$O$_3$	MgO	CaO	Na$_2$O	K$_2$O	P$_2$O$_5$	SO$_3$	Total
Basalt	46.02	3.13	13.58	16.23	0.23	5.46	10.14	2.55	0.81	1.06	0.79	100
Rhyolite	77.32	0.16	11.72	1.90	0.07	0.22	0.94	3.10	4.56	0.02	0.00	100

2-9. Analysis of rhyolite and basalt. These are volcanic rocks containing silica and alumina. Rhyolite is a fine-grained, light-colored silicate rock. Basalt is a dark silicate rock with lower silica and much higher iron, calcium, and magnesium.

Geology

2-10. Matt Fiske's lava oil spot bottle and cups, to 15 in. (38 cm) in length, fired twice: once to cone 12 in oxidation, the second time in a complicated reduction/oxidation cycle. Vesicular basalt slab from locally prospected lava rock, Sid Butte, Idaho, Snake River Plain, 2015. *Image: Courtesy of the artist.*

2-11. Bjarni Sigurdsson's vases, to 5½ in. (14 cm) in height, stoneware glazed with ash from the Icelandic Eyjafjallajökull volcanic eruption in 2010.
Image: Courtesy of ABC Carpet and Home, New York, New York.

have banded, folded or layered structures. Talc, a magnesium silicate mineral commonly used in glazes, forms a type of schist known as soapstone or steatite under pressure.

Over time, rocks are brought to the surface by earth movements and eroded, broken down and transported by glaciers, rivers, and the wind and deposited in lakes and estuaries as sediments (2-12). Sedimentary rocks include sandstone, limestone, and chalk, which was built up from layers of fossil shells and plankton deposited in warm Cretaceous seas over millions of years (creta is chalk in Latin). Embedded in the chalk are nodules of flint, thought to be derived from ancient siliceous sponges. Most clays are also sedimentary deposits, composed of weathered granites. When clay is covered with new sediments and compressed over millions of years, it gradually turns into shale. When shale is compressed and heated, it changes into slate. Rocks are continually recycled, so that ancient shales are weathered and transported to produce new layers of sedimentary clay. Shale can also be turned back into plastic clay by crushing and blunging with water.

Geological Time Scale

When British geologists began to study rock layers, they discovered that the oldest rocks exposed at the surface were in north west Scotland and the youngest were in

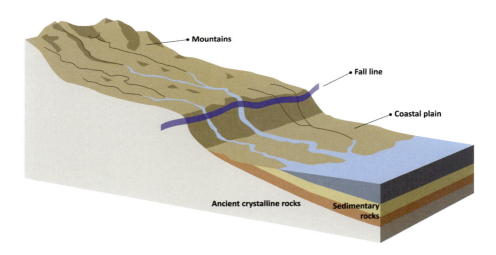

2-12. Diagram of the fall line and coastal plain. The crystalline rocks in the mountains are eroded and sedimentary clay is deposited at the fall line and on the coastal plain.

south east England. This is because the south east of England is gradually subsiding. In between, there is a sequence of layers of rocks and sediments, which were laid down over time. It is useful to list the rock layers, or strata, in the order in which they were deposited. We will look at various potters' materials, starting with the oldest to be formed. The relevant materials are listed in the table (2-15) and shown on the maps of the US and UK (2-13 and 2-14). Geological time periods from the Precambrian (up to 2.5 billion years ago) through the Carboniferous, Jurassic, Cretaceous, and up to the last Ice Age ending around twelve thousand years ago are covered. The Cambrian and Devonian geological periods were named after Cambria (Wales) and Devon (a county in England) by the British geologists who first surveyed the rock strata.

Old Rocks: Precambrian to Devonian

Geologists can date rocks by measuring the relative amounts of radioactive minerals present in the rocks. Some of the oldest rocks used in the ceramics industry are nepheline syenite from Ontario, Canada, formed 1.3 billion years ago and metamorphic talc and wollastonite from the Adirondack mountains in north-eastern New York state, formed more than 600 million years ago. Fossils found in sedimentary layers also help to date rock deposits. Similar trilobite fossils found in Scotland and North America showed that they were once joined together, 500 million years ago. Around that time, plate movements in the Earth's crust caused the uplift of a range of mountains stretching from North America, through Scotland to Norway. The tectonic plate covered by the ancient Iapetus Ocean (which lay between Norway and Canada) was subducted beneath the North American plate, the sea closed up and Scotland and England collided. The Caledonian mountains were at their highest around 400 million years ago in the Devonian period, when they weathered to produce large deposits of sandstone, known as the Old Red Sandstone as it often contains red iron oxide. Sandstone and metamorphic quartzite are also found in the Appalachians and in the Midwest, US. Sandstone is easier to break up for grinding than the large quartz crystals found in rock veins. Clays were also deposited during this period but over time they became covered by subsequent deposits and compressed into shale and slate.

Coal and Fireclay: Carboniferous Period

During the Carboniferous period 350 million years ago, deposits of coal were formed from ancient swamps. Sedimentary clays from weathered basalt were also laid down in

2-13. Map of North America showing commercial clay and feldspar deposits.

Geology

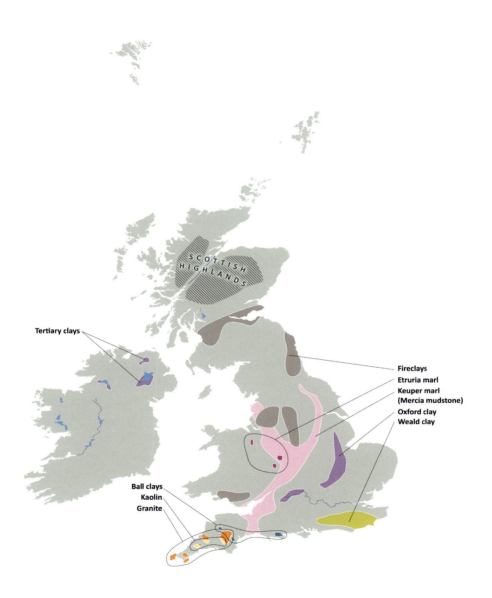

2-14. Map of Britain and Ireland showing commercial clay and granite deposits.
Images 2-13 and 2-14: Henry Bloomfield.

layers with the coal. This occurred in Staffordshire, England, where red Etruria Marl is found overlying coal seams, as well as in Missouri and Ohio in the US, where fireclays are mined. Geological maps show strikingly that the six pottery towns of Stoke-on-Trent in Staffordshire were built along the line where the red clay seam meets the surface. During the eighteenth century, potters also started to bring in flint from south east England, ball clays from Dorset, and kaolin from Cornwall (and some from North Carolina), but still used the locally available fireclay for saggars and coal for firing. They used chert, a local silica rock, to make millstones to grind the calcined flint and bone ash used in the white clay bodies.

Similar clays were deposited in the Pennsylvania and Mississippi lowlands in the US. Carboniferous deposits of fireclay, coal, and red clay are found in Oak Hill, Ohio, where Cedar Heights Redart earthenware clay and Cedar Heights Goldart fireclay are mined by the Cedar Heights clay company. The fireclay in southern Ohio was discovered in the mid-nineteenth century by a firebrick maker from Wales, although it had also been used by the Paleo-Indian Americans. The yellow clays of eastern Ohio were used from the 1840s by immigrant potters from Staffordshire. The main centers of the American pottery industry that developed from around that time were in East Liverpool, Ohio and Trenton, New Jersey. There were also individual potters working in many areas where there was locally available clay, such as the Shenandoah Valley in Virginia and Catawba Valley in North Carolina.

Other clays deposited in later periods include the Triassic red Keuper Marl in the English Midlands and the Jurassic Oxford clay, which is high in carbon and used to make bricks. The carbon acts as fuel and enables the bricks to be fired more economically. Marl clays can be high in iron and calcium and often fire a pink or buff color. They were used by seventeenth century English potters making tin-glazed earthenware. In Northern Ireland, brick and pipe clays were mined around Lough Neagh in the east and Lough Erne in County Fermanagh to the west, where Belleek Pottery was set up in the mid-nineteenth century. These types of clay are very common and found in many lowlands, lakes, and rivers.

Feldspar Formation

In Cornwall, England, 300 million years ago, a large granite batholitic intrusion (magma dome) formed underground. Hot gases caused the formation of minerals including tin and copper ores, which were mined from the Bronze Age (2150 BCE) until the twentieth century. More importantly for potters, this granite decomposed to form Cornwall Stone and pure white kaolin (3-1).

In North Carolina and South Dakota, granites and coarse-grained pegmatites were formed. These are important sources of sodium, potassium, and lithium feldspars. The North Carolina soda feldspar mine is at Spruce Pine in the Appalachians. Potash feldspar is mined in the Black Hills in South Dakota, which are formed from very old, Precambrian granites and pegmatites. The hills were explored by George Armstrong Custer and gold was found in 1874, two years before he was killed in Custer's Last Stand at the battle of Little Bighorn. Custer feldspar has been mined there since 1928. Its composition is kept constant by blending ores from a number of different mines throughout the hills.

Bentonite and Stoneware: Cretaceous Period

During the Cretaceous period 135 million years ago, volcanic ash rich in iron and magnesium was deposited and transformed into bentonite clays in the Benton Shale, Wyoming, not far from the Black Hills where Custer feldspar is mined. The name bentonite now refers to a very plastic type of clay (see Chapter 3). The Great Plains of North America were covered by an inland sea during that time and bentonite deposits were formed around the edges of the Black Hills and in the Bighorn Basin to the west.

Further north, in Canada, a range of stoneware clays is mined near Ravenscrag in southern Saskatchewan by Plainsman Clays. The clays are part of the Whitemud formation, deposited when the Rockies were weathered and layers of clay were washed down onto the plains, which were still covered by the Cretaceous inland sea. On the east coast of America in New Jersey, the South Amboy fireclay was deposited near Staten Island and later used by early American stoneware potters.

At the same time in south-east England, which was also covered by a warm sea, chalk deposits were formed, containing layers of flint nodules along what was once the sea bed. During the same period, the Weald and Gault clays were also deposited, which have been used to make bricks locally in Kent and London but have a high calcium content so are not suitable for stoneware as they melt at high temperatures.

The Great Extinction

Sixty-five million years ago, the great extinction occurred and the dinosaurs on the land and the ammonites in the sea died out. This is the major extinction event thought to have been caused by an asteroid striking Earth and can be seen in the rock strata, where it is known as the K-T (Cretaceous-Tertiary*) boundary, below which dinosaur fossils are found. Their fossils can be found in the limestone

Era	Million years ago	Major Epoch	Formation of Various Potters' materials.
4	Recent up to 0.012	Holocene	
	up to 1.6	Pleistocene	Ice age. Iron-rich clay Fremington/Albany slip
3	up to 5.3	Pliocene	Boron-rich hot springs in California
	up to 23	Miocene	Lithium in Atacama salt flats, Chile
	up to 36.5	Oligocene	Ball clay Devon UK
	up to 53	Eocene	Ball clay Dorset UK/ Tennessee, Kentucky US Kaolin Georgia, Florida US
	up to 65	Paleocene	The Great Extinction. Atlantic Ocean widens.
2	up to 135	Cretaceous	Chalk, flint, clay SE England. Whitemud formation, Canada. Bentonite Wyoming
	up to 205	Jurassic	Ammonites/Dinosaurs. Limestone, Oxford clay
	up to 250	Triassic	Keuper Marl Midlands UK
1	up to 290	Permian	Cornwall Stone and Kaolin in UK, Pegmatite North Carolina
	up to 355	Carboniferous	Clay/coal layers. Sandstone. Limestone.
	up to 410	Devonian	Old Red Sandstone
	up to 438	Silurian	Caledonian/Appalachian mountain ranges uplifted
	up to 510	Ordovician	Scotland still attached to North America
	up to 570	Cambrian	Trilobites appear
0	up to 2500	Precambrian	Talc, wollastonite NY. Nepheline syenite Ontario. Custer feldspar, South Dakota

2-15. Geological timeline of the formation of various potter's materials. Based on Richard Fortey's dates in his book *The Hidden Landscape*, 1993.

deposited during the Jurassic period, named after the Jura Mountains in the French Alps. At the same time, the continents of North America and Europe began to drift apart as the Atlantic ocean widened.

*The Tertiary era (now known as the Paleogene) began 65 million years ago.

Ball Clays

Many ball clay deposits were laid down between 35 and 50 million years ago when kaolin was washed into lakes and lagoons. This occurred in Devon and Dorset in England, as well as Kentucky and Tennessee in the US. The clays were often deposited in lenticular (lens shaped) sediments, together with sand and gravel. The sand is heavier and is usually found at the bottom of the deposit, while the carbon-rich organic matter is near the top. In Georgia and Florida, secondary kaolin deposits were washed down to the coastal plain. These deposits remained relatively white and pure, but contain more titanium than primary English china clay. There are also secondary kaolin deposits west of the Rocky Mountains in Helmer, Idaho and Ione, California.

Glacial Clays

The latest clays to be deposited, during the ice age which ended 12,000 years ago, were iron-rich red earthenware clays including Fremington clay in Devon and Albany slip in New York, supplies of which have now been used up, although there are alternative red earthenware clays available.

Minerals useful to potters which formed relatively recently include borates in desert hot springs and lithium in salt flats, which were formed from dried up paleolakes containing soluble minerals leached from rocks uplifted in the Andes mountain range. The mountains prevented the salt water from reaching the ocean, so it was trapped in the lake basin and slowly dried up.

The study of the formation of rocks and minerals can give insight into how glazes form in the kiln, as stoneware glazes are made from the same minerals: feldspar, limestone, and quartz (2-16, 2-17). Glazes form crystals while molten in the same way as rocks, depending on a slow rate of cooling for a large crystal size (6-6).

MINERALS

Rocks are aggregates of minerals. Some rocks, like chalk, contain only one mineral (calcite), while others such as granite are composed of several minerals (feldspar,

2-16. Matthew Blakely's *Dartmoor Granite Sphere*, 7 in. (18 cm) in diameter, clay made from kaolin and quartz derived from the same granite, glaze made from macrocrystalline gray granite found on Dartmoor, Devon, England, wood fired, 2014.

quartz, and mica). Most minerals have an ordered atomic structure and form crystals. There are a few exceptions, including opal, which is an amorphous silica glass containing water. Native elements such as gold, silver, and copper do not usually form crystals. However, many minerals used by potters are crystalline, including feldspar, kaolin, quartz, and dolomite. Minerals are often mined as impure rock ores, purified and powdered for use in the ceramics industry. Some minerals are much more variable than others. Minerals which are composed of several variable compounds, such as feldspar and rutile, can have a wide range of compositions and may also include impurities. However, minerals consisting of only one type of oxide such as quartz are likely to be fairly pure. Minerals have specific ratios of metal atoms to oxygen atoms,

2-17. Matthew Blakely's *Carved Edinburgh Sphere*, 10 in. (26 cm) in diameter, high-iron secondary kaolin stoneware, glaze made from rock found in Edinburgh, Scotland, wood fired, 2015.

for example quartz is always SiO_2, having one silicon atom to every two oxygen atoms. The shape of the crystal depends on the valence of the atoms and the relative atomic sizes (see Chapter 1 on crystal structure)

Feldspar

The first molecule in the formula is potassium-sodium oxide. The next is aluminium oxide or alumina. Finally, there are six molecules of silica. This is the way potters write the formula, showing numbers of molecules of alumina and silica. Chemists and geologists would write $(K,Na)AlSi_3O_8$, which means the same but adds all the oxygen atoms together at the end. This is the theoretical formula for feldspar but in naturally occurring feldspars there is a wide variation, arising from the different conditions the feldspars were formed under. Some types of feldspar, including Cornwall Stone and petalite, have a formula with eight molecules of silica to one of alumina.

> $KNaO \cdot Al_2O_3 \cdot 6SiO_2$
> K is the chemical symbol for potassium, Na is sodium, O is oxygen.

Feldspars make up more than 60% of the Earth's crust. There are several types of feldspar. As well as silica and alumina, feldspars used by potters in glazes usually contain both sodium and potassium. Particular alkali feldspars are usually named potash or soda feldspar, depending on which is the dominant alkali. Pure soda feldspar is known as albite (it is white) and has the formula $Na_2O \cdot Al_2O_3 \cdot 6SiO_2$, while pure potash feldspar is known as orthoclase, $K_2O \cdot Al_2O_3 \cdot 6SiO_2$ and can be white or pink. Most feldspars used by potters are a combination of these two alkali feldspars. Calcium feldspar is named anorthite and has the formula $CaO \cdot Al_2O_3 \cdot 2SiO_2$. It has a higher melting point and occurs in rocks associated with darker-colored silicates, so is less often used in ceramics. The general name used by geologists for mixed soda-calcia feldspar is plagioclase feldspar. Various feldspars come from different mines (e.g. Custer feldspar from South Dakota) and when they run out or become uneconomical to mine, they cannot always be replaced, except by combining other materials to make the same chemical formula. If potters rely on a feldspar from a particular source and it varies in composition from batch to batch or becomes unavailable, they can replace it with another feldspar and adjust other materials in the glaze to compensate (see Chapter 5 on glaze formula).

Cornwall Stone is a type of partially decomposed granite containing potash feldspar and is also high in silica. It is no longer mined, but potters' suppliers make a similar material by combining other feldspars. It is almost a glaze in itself when fired to stoneware temperatures and, together with kaolin, is also a component of porcelain clay bodies. Other materials such as volcanic ash, rhyolite, and granite may be substituted for feldspars.

Cornwall Stone Substitute	
Wollastonite	3
Custer feldspar	19
NC-4 feldspar or Minspar	45
EPK kaolin	11
Silica	22

Feldspars are very abundant minerals, mined as granites, pegmatites, and feldspar sands. They are found in many areas, including North Carolina in the US, Finland, and Norway. NC-4 Feldspar (now known as Minspar) is a soda feldspar from Spruce Pine, North Carolina. Custer feldspar is a potash feldspar from the Black Hills in South Dakota. In the US, feldspars are distinguished by brand names, however, in the UK, they are usually given the generic names Potash feldspar and Soda feldspar and are often sourced from Scandinavia.

Variants of Feldspar

Nepheline syenite ($K_2O \cdot 3Na_2O \cdot 4Al_2O_3 \cdot 8SiO_2$) is a feldspathic rock high in sodium, but with more alumina and less silica than other feldspars. Nepheline syenite is mined in Blue Mountain in Ontario, Canada and North Cape in Norway.

Petalite ($Li_2O \cdot Al_2O_3 \cdot 8SiO_2$) is similar to feldspar in composition, although it is higher in silica, like Cornwall Stone. Lithium is found in the pegmatite minerals petalite, spodumene, lepidolite, and amblygonite. Spodumene ($Li_2O \cdot Al_2O_3 \cdot 4SiO_2$) is a type of pyroxene, lower in silica than feldspar. Lepidolite ($Li_2F_2 \cdot Al_2O_3 \cdot 3SiO_2$) is a type of mica, a glittery, platy mineral that is more difficult to grind than feldspar and also contains fluorine. Amblygonite ($LiAlF \cdot PO_4$) is a lithium alumino-phosphate, also containing fluorine. Lithium carbonate can be extracted from these minerals but is expensive and is slightly soluble in water. It is cheaper to extract lithium from brine in salt flats such as those in Atacama, Chile.

Calcium

Limestone (2-18) is calcium carbonate ($CaCO_3$), known in its powdered form as whiting. Chalk is a very pure form of limestone, found in the white cliffs of south east England (2-19). Others forms of limestone may contain some magnesium carbonate. An alternative calcium mineral is wollastonite, calcium silicate ($CaSiO_3$). Wollastonite is mined in north eastern New York, Finland, and China. It is more expensive than whiting but is preferred in the ceramics industry as it produces no bubbles of carbon dioxide on firing. However, some studio potters' glazes, such as celadon, are enhanced by the presence of small bubbles, which give opacity and depth.

Calcium is also found in bone ash, calcium phosphate $Ca_3(PO_4)_2$, and wood ash, particularly soft wood ashes, such as those from pine, beech or apple trees (see chapter 8). The calcium phosphate mineral, apatite is also mined but contains fluorine and chlorine so is not used much by potters owing to the gases emitted on firing.

Magnesium

Talc is hydrated magnesium silicate ($3Mg \cdot 4SiO_2 \cdot H_2O$ containing bonded water), and is the major constituent of steatite or soapstone, a metamorphic rock, derived from magnesium-rich pyroxenes ($Mg_2Si_2O_6$) crushed and folded in mountain ranges such as the Adirondacks in north east New York state. Dolomite is a mineral

2-18. Limestone from the Zugspitze, Wetterstein range, Austria, Northern Alps, 2½ in. (6 cm) in length.

2-19. Chalk washed up in the River Thames, London, SE England, 3½ in. (9 cm) in length. Chalk is ground up to make whiting, or calcium carbonate.

containing both calcium and magnesium carbonate (CaCO$_3$•MgCO$_3$) named after a range of mountains in the Italian Alps. Used in glazes in small amounts (5%), dolomite and talc help to prevent crazing as they have low thermal expansion. They are used in larger amounts (20%) to make satin matte glazes. Light magnesium carbonate is used to make shrink-and-crawl glazes. Cordierite is an alumino-silicate containing magnesium, used to make fireproof clay bodies.

Barium and Strontium

Barium is found in the mineral barite (barium sulphate BaSO$_4$), which was used by Josiah Wedgwood as a flux in his colored Jasperware clay body. Barium sulphate is given to patients in a 'barium meal' to X-ray the intestines. It is non-toxic because it is insoluble, but it gives off sulphur dioxide on firing so barium is used in glazes in the form of barium carbonate (witherite), which is toxic. Strontium is mined as celestine (strontium sulphate) and converted into strontium carbonate for use in glazes. The mineral strontianite is strontium carbonate but it is less commonly mined. It is used as a non-toxic substitute for barium carbonate and it has properties similar to both barium and calcium carbonate.

Zinc

The main ore of zinc is zinc-blende or sphalerite (zinc sulphide ZnS). Zinc oxide can be used as a flux in mid-range glazes. It is an essential component of zinc silicate crystalline glazes. It prevents crazing but reacts with chromium-based colors, turning them brown. Zinc oxide glazes should not be fired in reduction as the oxide is reduced to the metal zinc, which is volatile at 1742°F (950°C).

Boron

Boron is found in colemanite (calcium borate 2CaO•3B$_2$O$_3$•5H$_2$O) and Gerstley borate (which contains ulexite, a sodium-calcium borate mineral). Gerstley borate is no longer mined but substitutes such as Gillespie borate are available. Borates form in hot springs and are found in evaporated lake basins in California and Turkey. However, these materials are slightly soluble and can cause gelling problems in the glaze bucket. Frits containing boron are also available and are less soluble. Calcium borate frit or Ferro frit 3134 is high in boron and is similar in composition to colemanite. Boric oxide is a powerful flux and a glass former and can also help to prevent crazing.

Silica

Silica (SiO$_2$) is found mainly in quartz (2-20), flint, and sandstone. It is the main glass former in glaze, and also in vitrified stoneware and porcelain. Secondary sources of silica include feldspar, clay, wollastonite, talc, frits, zirconium silicate, and wood ash. Grass ash contains more silica than wood ash.

Alumina

The main source of alumina (Al$_2$O$_3$) is clay, usually in the form of kaolin, ball clay or bentonite. It can also be found in its pure form in alumina hydrate (gibbsite) and is present in feldspar and kyanite, a metamorphic rock composed of alumina and silica and used as grog in clay bodies. Clay is the material most often used to supply alumina in glazes as it helps to suspend the glaze particles in water and improves the dry strength of the glaze. Alumina makes the glaze stiff and viscous in the melt and also inhibits the growth of crystals in the glaze.

2-20. Quartz from rock vein, 4 in. (10 cm) in length.

COLORING OXIDE MINERALS

The coloring oxides are the transition metal oxides used to color glazes and clay bodies (2-21). They are also used to make commercial ceramic stains.

Cobalt (Co)

Cobalt occurs in minerals such as skutterudite (2-22) and smaltite, together with nickel and arsenic, and is toxic. The cobalt oxide supplied to potters is a mixture of Co_3O_4 and CoO. It is a black powder (2-23), which changes to blue on firing in a glaze. It is

2-21. Heather Knight's (Element Clay studio), nesting scallop bowls, 8½ in. (22 cm) in diameter, porcelain with copper turquoise glaze. *Image: Courtesy of the artist.*

a very strong colorant and only a small amount is needed (0.1–2%). Cobalt carbonate $CoCO_3$ (2-24) is a pink powder which is two-thirds the strength of the oxide, so (1.5x) more is needed in the glaze recipe. Cobalt chloride, sulphate, and nitrate can be used to give watercolor effects but they are soluble in water and therefore more toxic. Cobalt gives a very strong blue in glazes, which can be subdued by adding iron and manganese.

Science for Potters

2-22. Cobalt nickel arsenide, mined as an ore of cobalt and nickel. First discovered in Skuterud Mines, Norway in 1845.

2-23. Black cobalt oxide.

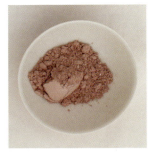

2-24. Pink cobalt carbonate.

2-25. Hydrated copper silicate mineral found together with other copper ores such as malachite and cuprite.

2-26. Black copper oxide.

2-27. Chrome diopside attached to quartz crystal. A chromium silicate pyroxene mineral, used as a green gemstone.

2-28. Chromium oxide.

2-29. Haematite. Red iron oxide mineral.

2-30. Red iron oxide.

Geology

2-31. Rhodonite. Manganese iron silicate, a pink mineral often found together with black manganese dioxide.

2-32. Pupurite. Manganese phosphate.

2-33. Manganese dioxide.

2-34. Annabergite. Hydrous nickel arsenate, an apple green mineral previously known as nickel ochre.

2-35. Vanadinite. Lead vanadate chloride mineral with hexagonal crystals.

2-36. Vanadium pentoxide.

2-37. Rutile. Titanium dioxide mineral with needle-shaped crystals, also found in beach sand deposits.

2-38. Rutile (titanium dioxide with up to 15% iron oxide).

2-39. Ilmenite (50% iron oxide and 50% titanium dioxide). *Images 2-22–2-39: Henry Bloomfield.*

61

Copper (Cu)

Copper is found in minerals such as malachite (copper carbonate) and chrysocolla (copper silicate) (2-25). Copper oxide CuO is a black powder (2-26), while copper carbonate $CuCO_3$ is green and is a weaker colorant. A small amount (0.5–3%) is used in glazes to give green or turquoise in oxidation and maroon red or pink in reduction.

Chromium (Cr)

Chromium is mined as iron chromite, $FeCr_2O_4$ and found in chrome diopside (2-27). Chromium oxide is supplied to potters as a green powder (2-28), Cr_2O_3, which is toxic. It is refractory (withstands high temperatures) and only small amounts (0.2–1%) will dissolve in a glaze. Chromium (0.1%) and tin (5%) will produce pink in glazes high in calcium. Chromium can also be used by potters in the form of iron chromate $Fe_2Cr_3O_{12}$ which gives gray or brown colors in glazes. The ending "ate," as in chromate, means that each chromium atom is combined with four oxygen atoms, two more than in compounds ending in "ite," as in chromite (compare the formula for iron chromite with iron chromate).

Iron (Fe)

Iron oxide is present in many rocks, minerals, and clays such as red earthenware clay. Yellow ochre (limonite), is a type of clay containing hydrated iron oxide while brown ochre (goethite) is a partially hydrated form. Sienna and umber are clay pigments containing iron and manganese. Iron oxide is available to potters as red iron oxide Fe_2O_3 (haematite) (2-29 and 2-30) or black iron oxide FeO. Magnetite, Fe_3O_4 is used to add speckle to glazes. It is hard to grind and the large particle size causes the speckles. Crocus martis is calcined iron sulphate, which is soluble in water and can be used to give watercolor effects. Iron oxide is used as a colorant in varying amounts (0.5–15%) in many classical Chinese glazes such as celadon, tenmoku, oil spot, and hare's fur.

Manganese (Mn)

The manganese ore is pyrolusite, MnO_2. It is supplied to potters as a dark brown powder. Manganese carbonate $MnCO_3$ is also available, the mineral ore of which is pink to brown and is called rhodochrosite. Other manganese minerals include rhodonite and purpurite (2-31 and 2-32). Manganese is used to make brown and black clay bodies and glazes (2-33). It is a relatively weak colorant so a large amount is needed (1–15%). The firing fumes from manganese are toxic.

Nickel (Ni)

Nickel oxide is available as black Ni_2O_3 or green NiO. It is found together with cobalt in ores such as nickeline (nickel arsenide) and annabergite (2-34). It is toxic and only a small amount is required in glazes (0.1–2%). It is often used in glazes to tone down other colors; with cobalt it will make gray, but will also produce pink, steel blue, and purple in barium-zinc glazes and mustard yellow and green with titanium in magnesium matte glazes.

Vanadium (V)

Vanadium is used together with zirconium silicate in commercial yellow and turquoise stains (2-35). It must be made into a stain before adding to the glaze to obtain these colors and is safer to handle in the fritted form. Vanadium pentoxide, V_2O_5 can be added directly to dry matte glazes and 2–8% will give mottled green or yellow (2-36). It is slightly water soluble and is toxic.

OPACIFIERS

Opacifiers make glazes opaque and white. They withstand high temperatures and do not completely melt in the glaze, remaining suspended in the glaze or re-crystallizing on cooling.

Tin (Sn)

Tin oxide, SnO_2 (cassiterite) is supplied to potters is a refractory white powder and additions of 5–10% will make glazes opaque. It may cause glazes to pick up a pink blush from volatile copper (in reduction) or chromium (in oxidation) in the kiln.

Zirconium (Zr)

Zirconium silicate (zircon, $ZrSiO_4$) is less expensive than tin oxide, but a larger quantity of 10–15% is required to fully opacify a glaze. It is used as a stabilizer in commercial stains, particularly high temperature reds and yellows.

Titanium (Ti)

Titanium dioxide, TiO_2 is found in the mineral anatase, as well as rutile (2-37 and 2-38) and ilmenite (2-39), both of which also contain iron oxide. Rutile contains up to 15% iron, while ilmenite contains 50% iron oxide. They are found together with zirconium in sedimentary deposits in beach sands. Impurities including vanadium and chromium may sometimes be present in rutile, causing a pink color with tin oxide. Titanium (2–10%) encourages crystals to seed in glazes and often forms mottled or streaked variegations. It will pick up color from iron in the clay body, so does not produce such white glazes as tin or zirconium.

Fig. 2-40. Tin oxide (right), fired in a glaze (left) makes the glaze white and opaque. It has a high melting temperature and the white particles stay suspended in the glaze rather than melting.

We have seen how minerals are formed and recycled in the Earth's crust. Aluminosilicates form the most important types of minerals used in ceramics: feldspars and clays. In the next chapter we will look at the structure and properties of clay.

US/UK Materials Substitutions

US	UK
Bentonite, Macaloid, Veegum	Bentonite
Cornwall stone	Cornish stone
Custer feldspar, G-200, K-200	Potash feldspar
EPK Edgar Plastic Kaolin	China clay
Ferro frit 3110	High-alkaline frit
Ferro frit 3124	Borax frit
Ferro frit 3134	Calcium borate frit
Ferro frit 3249	Low-expansion frit
Foundry Hill Creme	Buff stoneware
Georgia kaolin, 6 Tile kaolin	China clay
Cedar Heights Goldart	Fireclay
Helmer kaolin	China clay
Kentucky OM-4 ball clay	Hymod AT ball clay (high iron from Dorset)
Kentucky Stone	Hyplas 71 ball clay (high silica from Devon)
Kona F-4, NC-4, Minspar 200	Soda feldspar
Cedar Heights Redart	Etruria Marl, Keuper Marl
Silica	Flint, quartz
Tennessee ball clay	HVAR ball clay (Devon)
Zircopax, Superpax, Ultrox	Zirconium silicate

Fig. 2-41. US/UK material substitutions.

CHAPTER 3

Clay

Clays include the minerals kaolinite and bentonite. Shales are clays which have become compressed over time. They can be reconstituted, either by natural weathering or by crushing and mixing with water to make plastic clay. Clays differ in their particle size, impurities, plasticity, and firing temperature. Blended clay bodies combine naturally occurring clays with other materials to give the right mix of making and firing characteristics for the potter. Most potters choose between earthenware, stoneware, and porcelain. This chapter will explain the differences between their working properties.

TYPES OF CLAY

Kaolin is the whitest, purest form of clay, named after a high ridge near Jingdezhen in China where it was first mined to make porcelain. The theoretical formula* for kaolin is $Al_2O_3 \cdot 2SiO_2 \cdot 2H_2O$. This means that every molecule of alumina is combined with two molecules of silica and two of water. Kaolin was formed from weathered feldspar in decomposed

*The theoretical formula $Al_2O_3 \cdot 2SiO_2 \cdot 2H_2O$ or $Al_2Si_2O_5(OH)_4$ is the ideal chemical composition. Most clays will also contain impurities.

3-1. Kaolinized granite from Wheal Martyn, 2¼ in. (8 cm) in length, St. Austell, Cornwall. The white, powdery areas are kaolin. The piece of granite on the right is not kaolinized.

granite (3-1), such as in the deposit in Cornwall, England known as Grolleg or China clay. During the cooling of the magma forming the granite, hot gases containing boron and fluorine attacked the rock, forming the minerals tourmaline (a black boro-silicate), fluorspar (calcium fluoride), and topaz (an alumino-silicate containing fluorine) (2-6). At that point the rock became Cornwall Stone, a type of potash feldspar (3-1). From the theoretical chemical formula of this feldspar, $KNaO \cdot Al_2O_3 \cdot 8SiO_2$, you can see that it contains the alkaline oxides of potassium (K) and sodium (Na). From the formula for kaolin, $Al_2O_3 \cdot 2SiO_2 \cdot 2H_2O$, you can see that the alkalis have gone and there is added water. So when Cornwall stone is attacked by water vapor and carbon dioxide during weathering, feldspar is converted to kaolin plus alkali, and the alkalis are leached away, leaving kaolin, quartz, and mica. If found in the place where this is formed, it is known as primary clay and is more like a crumbly rock,

3-2. Fossiliferous clay, 4 in. (10 cm) in length, Bracklesham, West Sussex, England, Eocene (45 million years old).

3-3. China clay pit, Wheal Martyn, St. Austell, Cornwall. The crumbly white rock is exposed by blasting, then a powerful water hose is directed at the rock face to wash out the clay. The water is pumped from the bottom of the pit into settling troughs, where the quartz and mica are separated out.

3-4. Doble's clay pit, St. Agnes, Cornwall. This fireclay deposit lies on the north coast of Cornwall between the granite headland and the sea, directly under the thin topsoil. The gray refractory clay is dug out and mixed with ball clay to form the clay body used by the Leach Pottery.

from which the clay can be washed using water. The clay remains suspended in the water for longer than the quartz and mica, which gradually settle out (3-3).

Clay that has been transported and deposited by rivers, glaciers or the wind, is known as secondary clay (3-4). As the clays are transported, their particles are abraded and broken up into finer particles. They pick up impurities on their way, depending on the type of rock the river or glacier is flowing over. Georgia (6 Tile) and Florida (EPK) kaolins are secondary clays, which contain more impurities than primary kaolins and fire less white. However, as they have a finer particle size, they are more plastic than primary kaolin. Some sedimentary kaolins, such as Helmer kaolin from Idaho, contain more alkalis, titanium and iron oxide and can be used as flashing slips, creating an orange color when wood fired. There are several other types of secondary clay including ball clay, fireclay, and red earthenware clay.

Ball clay is a fine-grained, plastic, secondary clay. It is often gray in color owing to the presence of lignite (carbon), which burns out during firing. English ball clays are mined in Devon and Dorset and have higher dry strength but greater shrinkage than American ball clays. Kentucky ball clays have lower carbon, while those from Tennessee have lower iron content and fire whiter. Some ball clays can contain up to 25% quartz, also known as free silica (in addition to the silica chemically combined with the alumina in the clay structure). As well as carbon and iron, impurities in the clay can include titanium, calcium, magnesium, and potassium oxides. Titanium oxide in the clay body prevents translucency in porcelain and causes celadon glazes to appear green rather than blue. Ball clays are used in clay bodies to add plasticity.

Fireclay is a refractory type of secondary clay which has a large particle size and is high in alumina, so can be fired to high temperatures. It is found under coal deposits in the Midlands and Scotland in the UK, Missouri and Ohio in the US. Fireclays were formed from the earth in which the coal forests grew. They are high in alumina because it remains in the soil after the plants have absorbed the soluble alkalis and some of the silica. Fireclays may also contain carbon from lignite (coal) and sulphur from iron pyrite (3-5). The sulphur burns out as sulphur dioxide, leaving dark specks of iron oxide. Fireclay is used in stoneware clay bodies and also for making kiln bricks and shelves.

Owing to their very fine particle size, clays can be transported in rivers a long way and end up in lakes, lagoons, and estuaries. When the clay particles reach the sea, they become

3-5. Brownhills clay pit, South Staffordshire. *Image: courtesy of Potclays.*

flocculated (clumped together) by the salt water and are deposited. Marine clays often contain the remains of fossilized sea shells, so can be high in calcium carbonate (3-2). These marl clays can only be fired up to earthenware temperatures as the calcium acts as a flux at higher temperatures. Any large grains of calcium carbonate may explode in the kiln.

Red earthenware clays consist of illite and kaolin clays, quartz, and a considerable amount (6–10%) of red iron oxide. This means they melt at a lower temperature than other, lighter-colored clays. Some red clays, such as Fremington clay in North Devon, were carried there and deposited by glaciers during the ice age. Albany slip and Barnard clay were also formed by glaciers carrying weathered shales from the Appalachians.

Kaolin forms from weathered feldspar, while other types of clay are derived from the other components of granite or basalt. Muscovite mica weathers to form a type of clay called illite, named after the state of Illinois, found in iron-rich sedimentary clays such as Albany slip. Many ancient shales and red earthenware clays are composed of illite. The darker ferro-magnesian minerals from volcanic ash and basalt break down to form montmorillonite, or bentonite, named after the Benton Shale in Wyoming. Bentonite ($Al_2O_3 \bullet 4SiO_2 \bullet H_2O$) has the smallest particle size of all clays and so is very plastic and is used for adding plasticity to porcelain clay bodies and helping to suspend glaze particles in water. There are several types of bentonite, those high in sodium, which swell greatly in water, and others high in calcium, which swell less in water. Calcium bentonite is also known as Fuller's Earth, and is a useful adsorbent.

Typical Clay Analysis (%)

	China Clay	Fireclay	Ball Clay	Stoneware Clay	Red Clay (Etruria marl)
Alumina	44.0	41.0	37.5	32.0	21.5
Silica	53.0	55.5	56.5	63.0	65.5
Iron Oxide	1.0	2.3	2.0	2.2	9.5
Calcia/Magnesia	1.0	0.7	0.5	0.6	1.5
Potash/Soda	1.0	0.5	3.5	2.2	2.0

3-5. Typical clay analysis. *Information from* The Potter's Dictionary of Materials and Techniques, *by Frank and Janet Hamer, 2015.*

CLAY BODIES

Stoneware, Porcelain, Earthenware

Some clays can be used as dug from the ground, particularly red earthenware clays. They are usually mixed with water and sieved to remove stones and organic matter, before being dried to a usable consistency. Most clays, however, need to be blended with other clays to improve their working properties. Adding ball clay will improve plasticity, while fireclay will increase the firing temperature and china clay will make the clay whiter as well as more refractory (higher-firing). Fireclay sometimes contains iron pyrite, which adds speckle to the clay body. As well as clay, other materials can be added to change the color, texture, shrinkage, and hardness of the fired clay. Grog; ground, fired clay will reduce shrinkage and prevent warping and cracking while drying and firing. Grog is available in several different mesh sizes; from coarse (30–60 mesh) to fine (80–120 mesh). Molochite is a type of white grog made from china clay. Quartz and flint are added to clay bodies to increase hardness, while feldspar melts the silica in the clay and helps it to vitrify, as in porcelain. However, excess silica in the clay can cause dunting (cracking) during cooling in the kiln. Sand can be added to clays to give extra tooth and a pitted, orange peel effect in salt or soda firing. Granular feldspar can be added for texture, and melts into small white beads on firing, often seen in Japanese Shigaraki wood-fired pottery. Red clay or iron oxide are added to darken the color (3-6). Iron oxide fires to buff or red in oxidation and gray or brown in reduction. However, iron also acts as a flux in reduction and too much can cause slumping. Coloring oxides can be added to make a colored clay body. Manganese dioxide is used to color black clays but can give off toxic fumes in the kiln.

White clay bodies such as porcelain and white stoneware are made by mixing china clay, feldspar, quartz, and ball clay or bentonite (3-7). Porcelain is made from china clay and feldspar, together with some quartz and bentonite. White stoneware has more ball clay, is less white than porcelain and contains little feldspar so is not translucent. Clay bodies are mixed, sieved, and dried to a workable consistency. The larger particles of grog, sand or feldspar can then be added before putting the mixture through a pug mill, kneading, and wedging.

3-6. Stoneware clay: fireclay and ball clay mixed with red iron oxide, from WJ Doble, St. Agnes, Cornwall. This clay is used by the Leach Pottery in St. Ives.

3-7. Porcelain clay from Valentine Clays, Stoke-on-Trent.

Fig. 3-8. Charlotte Jones, Seaweed Lines vessel 33 in. (13 cm) in diameter, coiled pot using gabbro clay collected from the Lizard peninsula, Cornwall, copper oxide and white stoneware, burnished and high fired. *Image: Courtesy of the artist.*

Constituents of Clay Bodies

Material	Useful Properties	Disadvantages
Ball Clay, Bentonite	Plasticity, dry strength	High shrinkage
Fireclay	Refractory	
China Clay	White, refractory	
Stoneware Clay	Refractory	
Red Clay	Red or brown color	Low firing, porous
Feldspar, Bone Ash, Whiting	Flux, melter	Warping
Talc, Cordierite, Petalite	Flux for flameproof bodies	
Silica, Quartz, Flint	Hardness, vitrified	Dunting
Grog, Molochite	Open texture, low shrinkage	
Iron Oxide, Magnetite	Buff or brown color, speckle	Flux in reduction
Manganese dioxide	Black color	Toxic fumes

3-9. Table of constituent materials of blended clay bodies.

Clays are categorized according to their firing temperature (3-10). Earthenware clay is fired between 1742–2012°F (950–1150°C) and remains porous, so usually needs to be covered with a glaze to make it waterproof. Red earthenware can be fired slightly higher until it becomes non-porous. Some white earthenware bodies contain talc and will melt completely if fired too high. The advantage of earthenware is that it does not shrink too much on firing and feels light to pick up, but it is not as strong as stoneware and is more likely to chip and crack.

Stoneware is fired between 2192–2374°F (1200–1300°C) so that it becomes vitrified and non-porous. Stoneware clays shrink on firing by about 12%. They range in fired color from cream to buff in oxidation or gray to dark brown in reduction. Porcelain can be fired to stoneware temperatures or higher and is more likely to warp than stoneware. It shrinks by about 15% and becomes dense and glassy. It is blue-white in reduction or creamy white in oxidation and translucent if thin. Bone china is an English version of porcelain containing 50% bone ash. It is not very plastic and is formed into ware by slip casting in industry, where the bisque is fired to a high temperature to vitrify the clay body and the glaze is fired to a lower, earthenware temperature. Stoneware, porcelain, and bone china are much stronger than earthenware and do not chip or crack as easily. Porosity and strength are related; vitrification reduces porosity and increases strength (see chapter 8). The structure of clays will be explained in more detail in the next section.

Clay	Typical UK Composition (%)	Firing Temperature
Red Earthenware	Red clay	1742°–2102°F 950°–1150°C
White Earthenware	China clay 25, ball clay 25, feldspar 15, flint 35	1742°–2102°F 950°–1150°C
Stoneware	China clay 40, ball clay 40, feldspar 15, quartz 5	2192°–2372°F 1200°–1300°C
Porcelain	China clay 55, bentonite 5, feldspar 27, quartz 17	2282°–2552°F 1250°–1400°C
Bone China	China clay 25, feldspar 25, bone ash 50	2192°–2282°F 1200°–1250°C

3-10. Table of typical compositions of different UK clay bodies; earthenware, stoneware, porcelain, and bone china. Stoneware can also be made from ball clay and fire clay, but will be less white.

The Structure, Properties, and Chemistry of Clay

Clay is composed of flat, almost hexagonal plates with water in between (3-11). The plates can slide over each other but also stick together, so that the clay is plastic when wet. This means it can be shaped easily but also holds its shape, unlike an elastic material, which returns to its original shape when the force deforming it is removed. The particle size of clay is very small, particularly in sedimentary clays, which have been abraded during transport by rivers or glaciers. The smaller the particles, the more plastic the clay will be. Clays have much smaller particles than sand or silt, and are only a few thousandths of a millimeter wide (0.002 mm =2 μm). Clay crystals are roughly hexagonal in shape, similar to the related sheet minerals, such as mica, from which they are derived. Each tiny clay crystal consists of thousands of stacked atomic layers.

At the molecular level, clay is composed of alternating layers of silica, alumina, and water. The silica molecule has a tetrahedral shape, a triangular pyramid, with a silicon atom in the center and four oxygen atoms, one at each corner (3-12). Alumina molecules

3-11. Close up of kaolinite in Jurassic sandstone, UK North Sea, clay type confirmed by X-ray diffraction. Width of image: 20 microns across (50 images side by side would measure 1 mm). *Image: Evelyne Delbos, courtesy of The James Hutton Institute, reproduced from the 'Images of Clay Archive' of the Mineralogical Society of Great Britain and Ireland and The Clay Minerals Society.*

have an octahedral shape, two square-based pyramids joined together with an aluminium atom in the center and six oxygen atoms at the corners. Kaolin is the simplest type of clay. Alternating silica and hydrated alumina layers make up the structure of kaolin, $Al_2O_3 \bullet 2SiO_2 \bullet 2H_2O$ or $Al_2Si_2O_5(OH)_4$ (3-13). In a molecule of kaolin, four of the oxygen atoms are joined to a hydrogen atom. This means the alumina is hydrated or combined with water. This water is chemically bound in the clay structure, even when the clay is bone dry. The top of the alumina layer is composed of hydroxyl ions, OH^-, so although the kaolin molecules are bonded together strongly within the sheet, they are only weakly bonded to the sheets above and below. This enables them to slide easily over each other, which gives clay its plasticity. However, because of the strong bonds within the sheet, the kaolin particles are relatively large and so the plasticity of pure kaolin is low. Kaolin is the main constituent of china clay, ball clays, and fireclays. There is another clay mineral with same formula as kaolin, known as halloysite, which has tube shaped crystals and is used in Southern Ice porcelain.

Several other types of clay exist, which have slightly different structures. Illite (like mica) has three repeating layers: silica, alumina, then an inverted layer of silica, with

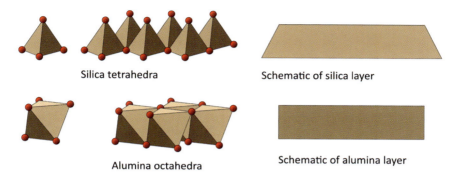

3-12. The structure of clay. Silica tetrahedra and alumina octahedra. The red atoms at the corners are oxygen. The silicon atoms are at the centers of the tetrahedra and the aluminium atoms are at the centers of the octahedra.

potassium ions bonding together each group of three layers (3-13). At the top and bottom of each group is a layer of oxygen atoms in a hexagonal structure, into which fit the potassium ions, K^+ (an ion is an atom or molecule which has lost or gained an electron). The layers in illite are therefore bonded together more strongly than in kaolin, which only has weak hydroxyl bonds between its layers. The potassium ions are attracted by an overall charge deficiency caused by substitution of some of the silicon atoms for aluminium and some of the aluminium atoms for magnesium or iron. These impurities can cause the clay to become colored. Illite clays often contain a large amount of iron oxide, and are used by potters as red earthenware. The iron oxide acts as a flux and reduces the firing temperature of the clay. The small particle size means that it is a very plastic clay, with good properties for throwing. Illite is thought to be an intermediate stage in the conversion of muscovite mica to kaolin or montmorillonite.

Montmorillonite (bentonite), like illite, has three repeating layers, but with water in between (3-13). The formula for bentonite is $Al_2O_3 \cdot 4SiO_2 \cdot H_2O$, which has twice as much silica as kaolin, as there are two layers of silica for every layer of alumina. Because the three-layer sheets are only weakly bonded together, with oxygen atoms at the top and bottom, additional water can easily get in between, which gives the clay its slippery feel. Some of the silicon atoms in bentonite are replaced by aluminium, and these in turn can be exchanged for magnesium and iron, which create an overall negative charge. Positively charged sodium or calcium ions are therefore attracted to balance the charge. Sodium bentonite can absorb a large amount of water, which causes it to expand greatly when added to water. This makes it very useful for suspending glaze ingredients in water.

It is also used in small amounts to increase plasticity in clay bodies. However, as some of the aluminium atoms are substituted by iron or magnesium, bentonite usually has more impurities than kaolin. Bentonite is more plastic and has greater dry strength but higher shrinkage than kaolin. The clay particles are much thinner than those of kaolin, less than a tenth of the thickness, like thin flakes rather than plates. This makes it extremely plastic. Calcium bentonite swells less than sodium bentonite, but it has the useful property of attracting organic molecules and is used as an adsorbent in cat litter.

Owing to the extra layer of silica, illite, and bentonite clays have higher silica than kaolin, which causes them to vitrify more than kaolin during firing (3-13). They also contain more iron oxide, which causes a buff, red or brown color on firing.

Many sedimentary clays contain a mixture of kaolin, illite, and montmorillonite, with layers repeating randomly. For example, Redart clay (from Cedar Heights Clay Company, Ohio, US) has the following composition: illite 40, kaolinite 10, mixed layered clays 15, quartz 30, red iron oxide 7. The structure and type of clay can be determined using x-ray diffraction, which measures the symmetry and spacing between the atomic layers. Kaolin has the smallest spacing and bentonite has the largest (3-13).

We have seen how the structure, particle size, and chemistry of clays affect their properties. In the next chapter we will investigate the constituents of glazes, and see how they interact when fired in the kiln.

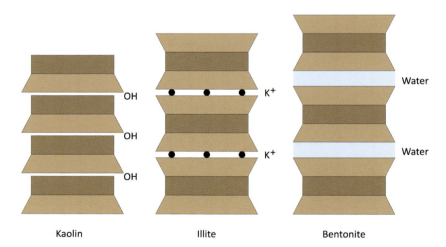

3-13. Layers of silica tetrahedra, alumina octahedra and water. Kaolin has repeating alumina and silica layers bonded with weak hydroxyl OH bonds. Illite has three layers bonded strongly with potassium (K$^+$) ions, while bentonite is similar but the layers are less strongly bonded and can swell by taking in water between each layer.

Clay

Gabbro clay collected from the Lizard Peninsula by Charlotte Jones, Cornwall.

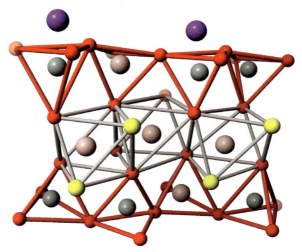
Detailed structure of mica and illite clay. Layers of silica tetrahedra and hydrated alumina octahedra. Purple atoms: Potassium, Red: Oxygen, Yellow: Hydrogen, Gray: Silicon, Brown: Aluminium. *Image: Courtesy of Elin Barrett.*

CHAPTER 4

Glaze

Potters have discovered empirically, through centuries of trial and error, how to make glazes. Master potters have passed their knowledge down through generations of apprentices and future generations can build on what has been learned in the past. This is why it is important for potters to share knowledge rather than keeping their techniques and recipes secret. In China, high-firing kilns were developed and potters must have noticed that wood ash falling onto pots produced a glassy surface. Gradually, they began to combine the ash with clay and feldspar and created glazes. The science of glazes has only been understood in the last hundred years. Hermann Seger was a German chemist and ceramics technologist who characterized glaze materials in the late nineteenth century. Seger determined the amounts of each material that should be used in a glaze and developed the Seger cone, a device for measuring heat in the kiln.

Pottery is glazed to make it durable, waterproof, and easy to clean, as well as decorative. Making glazes and adjusting the formulation of glazes to change their properties is a subject which many potters find daunting and this chapter will give a clear explanation of the materials and how they interact in a glaze.

COMPONENTS OF A GLAZE

Glazes are composed of three main constituents: glass former, flux, and stabilizer. The main glass former is silica, which makes a glossy surface when melted but has a high melting point, 3110°F (1710°C). In order to melt silica in a kiln, a flux must be added which lowers the melting point. The most commonly used fluxes are sodium, potassium, and calcium oxides. Together with silica, they make glass, although it would be too runny to use as a glaze. To prevent the glaze from running off the pot, alumina is added as a stabilizer. So, silica, fluxes, and alumina are the main components of a glaze.

Silica is the most common glass former used in glazes. Boron and

> **Defining The Terms**
> **Silica:** Glass former.
> **Flux:** Reduces the melting point of silica.
> **Alumina:** Stiffens the molten glaze.

phosphorus are also glass formers, but they are usually used together with silica to alter the properties of the glass, such as resistance to thermal shock. Fluxes include sodium, potassium, calcium, and barium. They are also known as network modifiers as they change the properties and fluidity of the glass. Stabilizers include alumina, titanium oxide, and zirconium oxide. They make the glaze more viscous when melted, and also more resistant to chemical attack. Metal oxide fluxes such as zinc and lead form part of the network in zinc silicate crystalline glazes and lead silicate earthenware glazes. They are also known as intermediates as their properties lie between those of network formers and fluxes.

Coloring oxides can be added to make colored glazes (see chapter 1). They react preferentially with titanium and tin oxide, then with boron, silica, other coloring oxides or fluxes in the glaze. Some coloring oxides act as fluxes (cobalt, manganese), while others make the glaze more viscous (chromium).

EUTECTIC: PHASE DIAGRAMS

There are three phases of matter: solid, liquid, and gas. Many substances which are solid at room temperature can be heated up until they melt to become a liquid, and then heated still further until they vaporize and become a gas (ice becomes water, which vaporizes to steam). However, when two materials are mixed together, the melting point of the mixture is often lower than that of either of the pure materials (for example, milk chocolate melts at a lower temperature than plain dark chocolate). This happens when silica and alumina are mixed in glazes. The melting point of silica is 3110°F (1710°C) and that of alumina is 3722°F (2050°C). At the eutectic point, when 10% alumina and 90% silica are mixed, the melting point is only 2813°F (1545°C). All other ratios of silica and alumina have higher melting points.

A phase diagram shows the different phases, primarily solid and liquid, and how they change with temperature. In the binary phase diagram for silica and alumina, shown in figure 4-1, the liquid mixture is at the top, the solid mixture at the bottom, and below the green "liquidus" line, solid silica plus liquid on the left and solid mullite ($3Al_2O_3 \cdot 2SiO_2$) plus liquid on the right. In these areas, melting takes place slowly, over a range of temperatures. However, at the eutectic point (the lowest-melting combination), complete melting occurs at a specific temperature. Mullite (named after the Isle of Mull in Scotland) grows in needle-shaped crystals during firing, and helps to vitrify the clay body and make the glaze-body interface, which gives strength to the fired pottery. Mullite does not form in the glaze but in or near the surface of the clay, where there is excess alumina available (4-1).

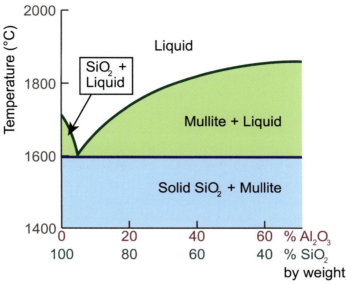

4-1. Simplified phase diagram for silica-alumina. The eutectic point is the lowest-melting combination of silica and alumina. Mullite is a compound of alumina and silica $3Al_2O_3 \cdot 2SiO_2$. Each phase is separated by a line: liquid, solid (blue) and mixtures of liquid with solid crystals (green).

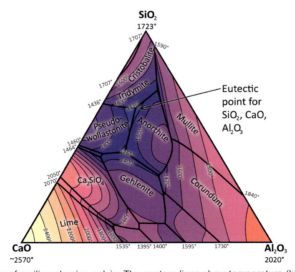

4-2. Phase diagram for silica-alumina-calcia. The contour lines show temperature (blue is relatively cool, red, and yellow are hot). The eutectic point is the lowest melting combination at 2138°F (1170°C). Lime is calcium oxide; wollastonite is calcium silicate, corundum is alumina, mullite is alumina-silicate, cristobalite and tridymite are silica phases, and anorthite is calcium feldspar. Note: The contour lines show temperature in °C.

The melting temperature can be lowered further by adding a flux, which forms a eutectic with the silica. The fluxes each form their own eutectic with silica and alumina, lowering the melting point. For example, 23.25% calcia, 14.75% alumina and 62% silica melts at 2138°F (1170°C). In practice, melting occurs over a range of temperatures. Potters usually mix silica, whiting, feldspar, and clay to make a transparent stoneware glaze. These melt together gradually, each oxide reacting with the other oxides, so alumina reacts with silica to form mullite; calcia reacts with silica to form wollastonite; alumina, silica, and calcia together form anorthite (calcium feldspar) (4-2). The precise eutectic melting point only occurs once the minerals anorthite, wollastonite (calcium silicate), and tridymite (high-temperature quartz) have formed. The lowest melting point occurs only when these minerals are mixed together in certain proportions. This eutectic is shown on a ternary phase diagram, with three axes instead of two. The contour lines show temperature, the lowest being at the eutectic point. Many stoneware glazes use several fluxes to give a better melt, including sodium, potassium, and calcium.

Silica-Alumina-Flux Eutectic Points

Alkali	Formula	Temperature °F	Temperature °C
Potassia	$K_2O \cdot Al_2O_3 \cdot SiO_2$	1283°	695°
Soda	$Na_2O \cdot Al_2O_3 \cdot SiO_2$	1350°	732°
Lithia	$Li_2O \cdot Al_2O_3 \cdot SiO_2$	1787°	975°
Alkaline Earth			
Calcia	$CaO \cdot Al_2O_3 \cdot SiO_2$	2138°	1170°
Baria	$BaO \cdot Al_2O_3 \cdot SiO_2$	2282°	1250°
Magnesia	$MgO \cdot Al_2O_3 \cdot SiO_2$	2471°	1355°
Strontia	$SrO \cdot Al_2O_3 \cdot SiO_2$	2552°	1400°

Fig. 4-3. Silica-alumina-flux eutectic points.

If the glaze has excess calcia, magnesia, baria, or strontia, it will no longer be at the eutectic composition and will not be transparent, as the excess will either remain unmelted or recrystalize on cooling. The glaze surface will be matte.

Glaze

STRUCTURE OF A GLAZE

Glaze has a network structure, composed of disordered silica chains, like glass (4-4). Glaze breaks like glass rather than cleaving like a crystal. The chains are linked together, like in a chain-link fence but less regular and in three dimensions (4-8). The silica chains are broken by fluxes such as sodium and potassium, which bond with the oxygen, thus preventing it from bonding with other silica molecules (4-7). Other fluxes such as calcium and magnesium help to stabilise the structure by forming a bridge between two silica molecules. The chains are cross-linked by alumina, which causes the glaze to become more viscous when melted (4-5). The difference in charge on the aluminium Al^{3+} ion (compared to silicon Si^{4+}) is balanced by sodium Na^+ or potassium K^+ ions. Aluminium, titanium, zinc, and lead can be substituted for silicon atoms in the chain (4-8).

Where glaze meets the clay surface, it seeps into the pores between the clay crystals and forms a body-glaze layer. This occurs more in stoneware and porcelain than in earthenware. At temperatures above 1832°F (1000°C), mullite crystals begin to grow at the body-glaze interface and help to interlock the glaze with the body, giving strength to the fired piece.

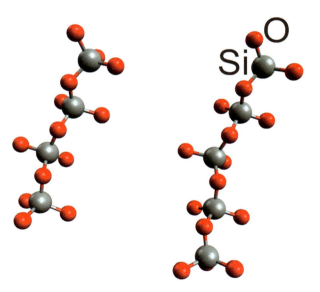

4-4. Chains of silica tetrahedra. Each silica tetrahedron has silicon at the center and oxygen at the four corners. In crystalline quartz, each oxygen atom is shared by two silicon atoms, giving the formula SiO_2. In a glaze, the silica tetrahedra are linked together in a randomly disordered three-dimensional network.

85

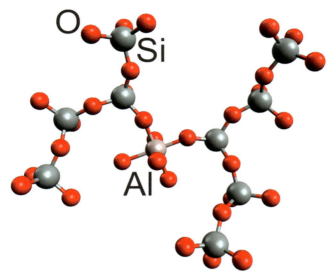

4-5. Alumina stiffens the glaze by cross-linking the silica chains.

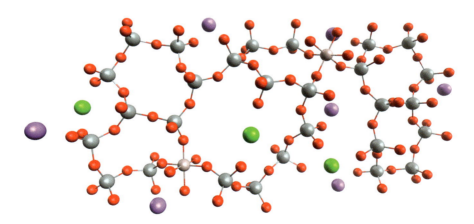

4-6. Imagine the glaze is a chain link fence. The flux atoms (purple sodium and green calcium) are like cannon balls bombarding the fence and breaking the links. This diagram is the conventional depiction of a glass or glaze structure. However, the flux atoms are bonded with silica via ionic bonds. The conventional diagram does not make this clear, hence diagram 4-8. Ball and stick diagrams are usually used to show covalent bonds such as Si-O. Covalent bonds are very stable and are directional. Ionic bonds such as Na-O are usually shown by $^+$ and $^-$ signs next to the Na and O atoms but some potters may not be familiar with this.

Glaze

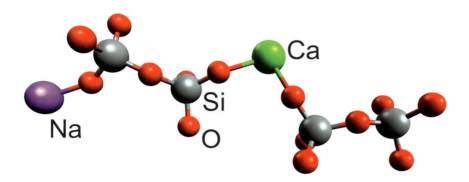

4-7. Sodium oxide forms the ends of chains, causing them to break from other silicon atoms. Calcium oxide forms part of the silica chain, linking silica tetrahedra and strengthening the glaze. Sodium and calcium form ionic bonds with oxygen, while silica and alumina are covalently bonded with oxygen. Ionic bonds are usually shown as separate Na⁺ and Ca²⁺ ions, but here the bonds with oxygen are shown for clarity.

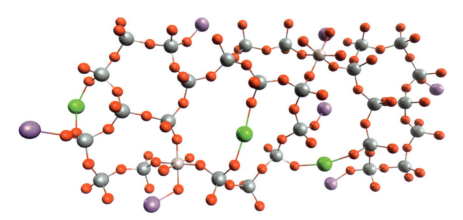

4-8. Diagram of glaze structure. The silica chains and alumina are joined by covalent bonds to oxygen, and form the network structure. Some of the silicon Si^{4+} ions are substituted by aluminium Al^{3+}. The difference in charge is balanced by sodium (Na^+) and calcium (Ca^{2+}), via ionic bonds with oxygen. These ionic bonds are less stable than the covalent bonds in the silica network.

4-9. Gray silicon, red oxygen, purple sodium, green calcium, and brown aluminium atoms.

87

CHAPTER 5

Glaze Formula

A glaze recipe can be reduced to a chemical formula. This makes it easier to compare with other glazes or to substitute different materials to obtain the same glaze recipe. There are many glaze formula calculation software programs, which potters can use to work out the glaze formula. However, it is useful to have an understanding of how glaze formulae are calculated and to be able to work out glaze material substitutions for your own glazes.

The glaze recipe shows the amount of each material by weight percent. This type of recipe is easy to read and is used for mixing a glaze batch from raw materials.

Clear Glaze
Cone 10

Whiting	20%
Feldspar	30
Kaolin	20
Silica	30
	100%

Each material in the recipe has a chemical formula.

Chemical formula

Whiting: $CaCO_3$
Feldspar: $KNaO \cdot Al_2O_3 \cdot 6SiO_2$
Kaolin: $Al_2O_3 \cdot 2SiO_2 \cdot 2H_2O$
Silica: SiO_2

The glaze formula is the sum total of all the oxides, in the same molecular proportions given in the glaze recipe (i.e. the recipe weight divided by the molecular weight). The water, H_2O, and carbon dioxide, CO_2 are given off in the firing. The glaze formula on the next page adds together the molecules in the recipe above. It is very similar to the formula for feldspar or Cornwall Stone, which is almost a glaze in itself if fired to a high temperature.

GLAZE FORMULA
$KNaO \cdot CaO \cdot Al_2O_3 \cdot 8SiO_2$

The table below shows a more precise version of this glaze formula known as the Seger unity formula or unity molecular formula, which shows the exact number of molecules of each flux, silica, and alumina (5-1). This is very accurate, but not the easiest notation to use in practical glaze development. The oxides are arranged in three columns; alkaline, amphoteric, and acidic. In the unity formula, the total of all the alkaline fluxes is made to add up to 1. This is almost the same as the simplified glaze formula above, but the quantities have been adjusted so that all the fluxes (K, Na, and Ca) add up to 1 molecule, so instead of 1 molecule of alumina and 8 silica, there are 0.5 alumina and 4 silica molecules. This enables direct comparison between glazes, regardless of the particular materials used in the recipe. The ratio of alumina to silica tells us something about the glaze properties. A ratio of 1:5 would give a matte glaze and a ratio of 1:8 gives a glossy glaze. In between matte and glossy are satin mattes, becoming gradually more glossy.

Glaze Unity Formula

Alkaline/basic (fluxes)	Amphoteric (alumina)	Acidic (silica)
K_2O 0.2	Al_2O_3 0.5	SiO_2 4.0
Na_2O 0.1		
CaO 0.7		
Total 1.0		

5-1. Glaze unity molecular formula.

HOW TO CALCULATE A GLAZE MATERIAL SUBSTITUTION
eg. Barium to Strontium Carbonate.

Similar glaze materials can be substituted in a glaze recipe, for example, barium carbonate can be substituted by strontium carbonate, which is not toxic. To calculate the weight of material needed to give the same number of molecules, the recipe weight should be divided by the molecular weight. Barium carbonate has a molecular weight of 197.3, while strontium carbonate has a molecular weight of 147.6 (obtained by adding the atomic weights of strontium, carbon, and three oxygen atoms, from the chemical formula $SrCO_3$, so less strontium will be needed to substitute for the barium, see appendix 1). The atomic weight is the combined weight of protons and neutrons. As different isotopes have different numbers of neutrons, the weight is averaged, which

5-2. Clockwise from top: bentonite, bone ash, Cornwall stone, dolomite, nepheline syenite.

explains why the atomic weights are not whole numbers. Dividing 147.6 by 197.3 gives 0.75, so the weight of strontium carbonate required to give the same number of molecules in the glaze is 0.75 times the weight of barium carbonate. A similar calculation can be made, for example, to find the amount of cobalt carbonate required to replace cobalt oxide in a recipe (in this case, around 1.5 times).

Some substitutions are more complicated, for example, whiting ($CaCO_3$) can be replaced by wollastonite ($CaSiO_3$), but the same number of molecules of silica must be subtracted from the total amount of silica in the glaze formula, as wollastonite contains both calcium and silica.

Other substitutions are very simple, for example, various feldspars are interchangeable weight for weight, although the glaze may change in character, depending on the composition of the feldspar. Naturally occurring minerals do not always have precise chemical formulae, but contain impurities which affect the material's properties. It is useful to know which glaze materials can be substituted for others as you may not have all the materials required in a particular recipe. If you are new to glaze making, it is only necessary to buy a few essential materials at first, including feldspar, whiting, silica, and china clay. If you are planning to make mid-range glazes, a borate frit such as Ferro frit 3134 will also be useful. Earthenware and raku glazes consist mostly of frit, with some clay and silica.

MATERIAL SUBSTITUTIONS

Potters' materials which can be used to replace materials which are unavailable (5-2 and 5-3).

Glaze Material Substitute

Glaze Material	Substitute
Barium carbonate x0.75	Strontium carbonate
Bone ash	Calcium phosphate
Cobalt oxide	Cobalt carbonate x1.5
Colemanite	Ferro frit 3134, calcium borate frit, P2954
Copper oxide	Copper carbonate x1.5
Cornwall stone	Custer feldspar and silica
Dolomite	Whiting and magnesium carbonate or talc

FFF feldspar	Custer feldspar and NC-4 feldspar
Gerstley borate	Ferro frit 3124, borax frit
Molochite	Bisque fired kaolin
Petalite, spodumene	Feldspar and lithium carbonate
Red earthenware clay	Iron oxide and clay
Rutile, ilmenite	Titanium dioxide and iron oxide
Soda feldspar	Nepheline syenite and silica
Talc	Magnesium carbonate or dolomite and silica
Wollastonite	Whiting and silica
Wood ash	Whiting and nepheline syenite

5-3. Material substitutions.

WHAT MAKES A STABLE GLAZE

Through trial and error, a set of limits has been determined, particularly for the amounts of silica and alumina in a glaze. Inside these limits, the glaze will be stable, insoluble and reasonably hard-wearing. It will be resistant to attack by acids in foods and alkalis in the dishwasher. However, many interesting glazes are outside these limits, such as copper red glazes, which have high alkali and low alumina. Matte glazes are likely to have lower resistance to attack by acids than shiny glazes. This is because matte surfaces are made up of microscopic crystals, which present more surface area for reaction with acids.

HARDNESS AND SCRATCH RESISTANCE

In general, it is better to use a mixture of several different fluxes than to rely on only one or two. Potash feldspar will make harder glazes with better scratch resistance than soda feldspar. The alkaline earths: calcium, magnesium, barium, and strontium will increase glaze stability, as will zinc oxide. Adding titanium or rutile will also help to improve resistance to acid attack. Adding zirconium silicate makes the glaze opaque and also improves durability and scratch resistance. Low alumina glazes may become scratched more easily than those within the limits for stability (5-4). In general, the higher the firing temperature, the harder and more durable the glaze will be, provided it contains enough alumina and silica. For earthenware and mid-range glazes, enough boron must be added to allow complete melting at the chosen firing temperature.

Matte and crystalline glazes may be marked by cutlery. This occurs when metal from the cutlery scrapes across and is deposited on the microscopically rough edges of crystals in the glaze. It is better not to use matte glazes on surfaces of functional pots that will come into contact with cutlery, although most marks can usually be removed. Zirconium opacified glazes may also by marked by cutlery, however, these marks may not be removeable.

LIMITS FOR STABLE GLAZES

To find out whether a glaze is within the limits for stability, its unity formula must first be calculated. There are many glaze calculation software programs available which can calculate the glaze formula for a given glaze recipe. The recommended amounts of alumina and silica in glazes increase with firing temperature. Glazes within these limits will be glossy glazes. Matte and crystalline glazes will often be outside these limits.

Alumina and Silica Limits

Cone number and temperature. Number of molecules in unity formula (5-4).

Cone 04	1940°F/1060°C	Al_2O_3	0.1–0.45	SiO_2	1.375–3.15
Cone 5	2192°F/1200°C	Al_2O_3	0.275–0.65	SiO_2	2.4–4.7
Cone 6	2237°F/1225°C	Al_2O_3	0.325–0.7520	SiO_2	2.6–5.15
Cone 8	2282°F/1250°C	Al_2O_3	0.375–0.75	SiO_2	3.0–5.75
Cone 9	2327°F/1275°C	Al_2O_3	0.45–0.825	SiO_2	3.5–6.4
Cone 10	2372 °F/1300°C	Al_2O_3	0.50–0.90	SiO_2	4.0–7.2

5-4. Alumina and Silica Limits (*Information from Cooper, Emmanuel and Royle, Derek,* Glazes for the Studio Potter, *BT Batsford Ltd, London, 1984.*)

Recommended Maximum Flux in Glaze Unity Formula

Cone	Temp °F/°C	MgO	BaO	ZnO	CaO	B_2O_3	K+Na
5	2192°F/1200°C	0.325	0.40	0.30	0.55	0.35	0.375
6	2237°F/1225°C	0.330	0.425	0.32	0.60	0.30	0.35
8	2282°F/1250°C	0.335	0.45	0.34	0.65	0.25	0.325
9	2327°F/1275°C	0.340	0.475	0.36	0.70	0.225	0.30
10	2372°F/1300°C	0.345	0.50	0.38	0.75	0.21	0.275

5-5. Recommended maximum flux in glaze unity formula (*Information from Cooper, Emmanuel and Royle, Derek,* Glazes for the Studio Potter, *BT Batsford Ltd, London, 1984.*)

Linda Bloomfield's three dimpled cups on a tray, 12 in. (31 cm) in diameter, praseodymium oxide and copper blue glazes, 2011. *Image: Henry Bloomfield.*

Science for Potters

CHAPTER 6

Glaze Fit

This chapter explains how important it is that the glaze fits the clay body. If the fit is not close, either the glaze or the pot may crack.

SILICA PHASES

As quartz is heated up, it changes in structure. The silica tetrahedra arrange themselves at slightly different angles to each other. The different forms are called phases. The silica phases include alpha-quartz up to 1063°F (up to 573°C), beta-quartz up to 1598°F (up to 870°C), tridymite up to 2678°F (up to 1470°C) and cristobalite, which eventually melts at 3110°F (1710°C) to form amorphous liquid silica. Tridymite and cristobalite each have their own alpha and beta phases. In the high-temperature beta phase, the bond angles between Si-O-Si are slightly straightened out. Once the silica has melted, the bonds are broken and the structure becomes disordered and is no longer crystalline.

If molten glaze is cooled quickly, the silica will stay amorphous and disordered like in a liquid. However, the clay body may still contain some crystalline silica and this will undergo the reverse phase transitions on cooling. The crystalline silica in the clay body not chemically combined in kaolin or feldspar is known as free silica. The solid silica crystals change volume when they change from one phase to another at a specific temperature. Each silica phase has a slightly different volume, and potters need to be aware of the inversion temperatures as they can cause dunting in the kiln.

QUARTZ AND CRISTOBALITE INVERSIONS

The two silica inversion temperatures important to potters, particularly when cooling the kiln, are the quartz inversion from beta to alpha at 1063°F (573°C) and the cristobalite inversion at 439°F (226°C) (6-1 and 6-2). The quartz inversion involves a 1% volume change and is a gradual change. The cristobalite inversion causes a sudden 3% volume change and can cause dunting if the kiln is opened at this stage. However, the cristobalite inversion can be useful in preventing crazing in glazed earthenware. This is known as the cristobalite squeeze as it contracts the clay body and compresses the glaze. Earthenware clay bodies can withstand this stress but not stoneware,

6-1. Alpha quartz structure. The Si-O-Si bonds are bent at an angle.

6-2. Beta quartz. The Si-O-Si bonds are straightened out, with an accompanying increase in volume.

particularly ovenware, which may be repeatedly heated to above 392°F (200°C), so cristobalite is not desirable in stoneware clay bodies. Fluxes in the clay body such as calcia and magnesia act as catalysts in the conversion of quartz to cristobalite. In stoneware and porcelain, more cristobalite forms the longer the ware is soaked or re-fired to high temperature, above 2012°F (1100°C). This may cause cracking when, for example, large plates are re-fired. The clay body suddenly changes in volume, but the glaze does not, causing stress and cracking of the plate.

GLAZE FAULTS AND HOW TO CORRECT THEM

For many potters, the first time they turn to a book like this will be when they need to resolve a glaze fault. Some faults, including crazing, cracking and shivering, are caused simply because the glaze does not fit the clay body used. It is important to understand how to modify the glaze in order to make it fit. Other problems such as pinholes and blisters may be caused either by under- or over-firing.

Crazing

Crazing occurs after the pot has cooled from the kiln, if the glaze is too small for the clay body (6-3 and 6-4). A network of fine cracks appears some time after the pot is removed from the kiln, accompanied by a series of pinging sounds. In earthenware, the cracks can cause the pot to leak. In all glazed ware, crazing greatly weakens the pot. Crazing can be corrected by adding materials with low expansion such as boron or reducing any high expansion materials such as feldspar. The list on page 100 shows

6-3. Oriental stoneware bowl with crazed celadon glaze. The craze lines have been stained black.

6-4. Porcelain test tile with crazed glaze.

glaze oxides in order of decreasing expansion. Low expansion materials such as borate frit, silica, clay or talc can be added a few percent at a time to a series of glaze tests. It is better to change one material at a time when trying to correct crazing. Also, it is simpler to alter the quantity of a material already in the glaze than to add a new component.

Shivering

Shivering is the opposite of crazing, when the glaze is too big for the clay body, and is a more serious fault. In earthenware and stoneware, slivers of glaze spontaneously chip off rims and the edges of handles. This can be dangerous to the user of functional ware. In porcelain, the glaze is more firmly bonded to the clay body and stresses between glaze and clay body can cause the pot to crack. Shivering can be corrected by adding high expansion materials to the glaze, such as alkaline frit or feldspar, which contain sodium and potassium. In the list of oxides below, high-expansion materials are at the top and low expansion at the bottom.

Expansion

High expansion
- Sodium oxide
- Potassium oxide
- Calcium oxide, strontium oxide
- Barium oxide
- Titanium oxide, lead oxide
- Lithium oxide
- Zinc oxide
- Magnesium oxide
- Tin oxide, zirconium oxide
- Alumina
- Silica
- Boron oxide

Low expansion

Crawling

Crawling occurs when the glaze cracks on drying and melts in the kiln to form beads with bare patches in between. It points to the glaze having its surface tension too high, e.g. in a similar way, water (high surface tension) will bead on a greasy surface, whereas soapy water (low surface tension) will coat it smoothly.

Crawling can be corrected by calcining materials with high drying shrinkage such as china clay and zinc oxide and reducing materials with high surface tension such as zirconium and tin oxide. The list on page 101 shows the oxides in order of decreasing surface tension, with high surface tension at the top and low surface tension at the bottom. The materials at the top of the list should be reduced if there are crawling problems. It may also help if the glaze is thinned with water, as thickly applied glaze can crack on drying. Dusty or greasy biscuit ware can also cause crawling. If this is the case, crawling can be prevented by sponging the biscuit ware and leaving to dry overnight before glazing.

Surface Tension

High surface tension
- Aluminium oxide
- Magnesium oxide
- Zirconium oxide
- Calcium oxide
- Tin oxide
- Zinc oxide
- Strontium oxide
- Barium oxide
- Silica
- Titanium oxide
- Boron oxide
- Lithium oxide
- Lead oxide
- Sodium oxide
- Potassium oxide

Low surface tension

Pinholes

Pinholes can occur in underfired or viscous glazes, where gases have escaped during firing but have not healed over (6-5). A soak at the top temperature for half an hour can help to smooth out the glaze. Pits left from grog removed during turning can also act as sites for pinholes. Sponging the clay surface after turning will prevent this. Some glaze materials such as zinc oxide can cause pinholes.

Blisters

Blisters sometimes occur in overfired glazes. They can cause sharp edges, which are unsafe to use on functional ware. Fluxes such as sodium oxide and borate frits become volatile above 2192°F (1200°C). Some glaze materials such as bone ash also give off gases. If the glaze is viscous, the gas bubbles may be trapped. Blisters can be ground down and refired.

6-5. Akiko Hirai's stoneware moon jar with pin-holed matte glaze.

SPECIAL EFFECT GLAZES
Many types of glaze faults can be made into a feature in special effect glazes such as crackle glazes, shrink-and-crawl lichen glazes, and volcanic glazes.

Matte
A shiny glaze can be made matte by saturating it with excess alumina, calcia or magnesia. The excess remains suspended in the glaze or forms tiny crystals, which give a matte surface texture. Alumina added in the form of clay can give a dry matte. Magnesia from dolomite or talc can give a very smooth, satin matte texture. Magnesium matte glazes are usually opaque and often have subdued color. Barium and strontium will give bright matte glazes with coloring oxides such as copper, cobalt and chromium. Titanium and zinc oxide can be used to make low-fired satin matte glazes.

Satin Matte Glaze	
Cone 8	
Talc	20%
Whiting	12
Zinc Oxide	3
Potash Feldspar	32
China Clay	16
Silica	17
	100%

Strontium Matte Glaze	
Cone 6–8	
Lithium Carbonate	3%
Strontium Carbonate	30
Zinc Oxide	3
Potash Feldspar	40
China Clay	6
Silica	18
	100%

Crystalline

Crystals often form in glazes which are low in alumina and contain excess calcia or magnesia. The lack of alumina in the glaze means that it is very fluid in the melt, and atoms can move around easily. Only a limited amount of calcia can dissolve in the glaze. The silica in the glaze reacts with the excess calcium to form crystals, which grow in the molten glaze if it is cooled slowly, which gives time for the atoms to arrange themselves in a crystal lattice structure (see chapter 1). These crystals can include wollastonite (calcium silicate $CaSiO_3$), diopside ($CaMgSi_2O_6$) and enstatite (magnesium silicate $Mg_2Si_2O_6$).

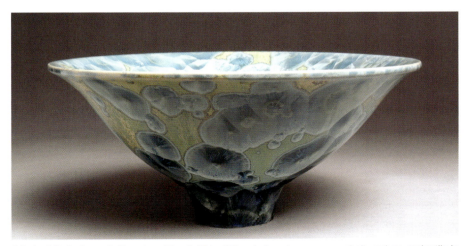

6-6. Avril Farley's crystalline glazed bowl, 12 in. (30 cm) diameter, copper, cobalt, cerium, and rutile in a zinc silicate crystal glaze. *Image: Courtesy of the artist.*

The latter two are types of pyroxene, a chain silicate (see chapter 2 on geology). The glaze becomes devitrified and is no longer transparent. There can be a few crystals floating in a matrix of glossy glaze, or the crystals can cover the entire surface to form a matte glaze if the kiln is cooled slowly. Barium, strontium and zinc will also form crystals in a similar way. Crystalline glazes with very large crystals can be made from zinc silicate if held for several hours during cooling at around 2012°F (1100°C) to allow time for the crystals to grow while the glaze is still molten. The zinc silicate mineral Zn_2SiO_4 is called willemite. Its crystals can be colored with cobalt, copper or nickel (6-6). The crystals selectively take up certain coloring oxide in preference to others. For example, cobalt will color the crystals blue, nickel will give steel blue and manganese will give pink only if there is no cobalt or nickel present. Manganese and copper oxide will usually color the background if there are other coloring oxides present. Titanium and rutile help to seed crystals. In a molten glaze, they initially form zinc titanate $ZnTiO_3$ or calcium titanate $CaTiO_3$, from which other crystals can grow on cooling. At stoneware temperatures, mullite in the glaze-body interface will act as a seed for crystals, as will the addition of wood ash or bone ash to the glaze.

Crystalline Glaze
Cone 8

Calcined Zinc Oxide	23%
Titanium Dioxide	4
Ferro Frit 3110	47
Calcined China Clay	3
Silica	23
	100%

Chun

Chun glazes have characteristic mottled opacity caused by tiny bubbles of phosphorus-rich glass suspended in the surrounding silica glass (6-7). The bubbles form a separate phase, which causes opacity and cloudy opalescence. Blue light is reflected more strongly than other colors of light by these tiny colloidal particles. The glaze itself is not blue, but it is an optical effect which makes the glaze look blue, particularly if applied thickly over a dark background, either a dark clay body or underlying iron-rich glaze. Phosphorus can be added to a glaze in the form of wood ash, bone ash, or calcium phosphate. A similar effect can be obtained using calcium borate frit (Ferro frit 3134) or colemanite. The addition of rutile or titanium also causes streaking and mottling in glazes. Chun-type glazes are usually very runny and should be applied thickly at the top of the pot and more thinly lower down.

6-7. Craig Edwards' *Memories of Sky #2*, 12 in. (30 cm) in diameter, local stoneware, tessha and chun glazes, NSW Australia, 2012. *Image: Stuart Hay.*

Chun Blue Glaze
Cone 9 Reduction

Talc	5%
Whiting	19
Calcium Borate Frit	9
Potash Feldspar	37
China Clay	2
Silica	28
	100%

Add:
Black Iron Oxide 1%

Copper Blue Glaze
Cone 6–8 Oxidation

Tin Oxide	5%
Whiting	14
Calcium Borate Frit	15
Soda Felspar	44
China Clay	5
Silica	17
	100%

Add:
Copper Oxide 0.1%

Shrink and Crawl

Materials with high shrinkage can be added to a glaze to cause it to crack and shrink on drying. Light magnesium carbonate, around 30% in the glaze recipe, will give this effect (6-8). The glaze must be applied thickly and care must be taken when handling so that the glaze does not flake off. Shino glazes which contain around 30% clay will also shrink and crawl slightly, giving a network of cracks.

Lichen Glaze (Mark Bell)
Cone 6

Material	%
Magnesium Carbonate	31%
Talc	8
Zinc Oxide	6
Frit P-25	6
Soda Feldspar	30
China Clay	19
	100%

6-8. Emma Williams' tall bowls, press-moulded black earthenware clay, barium and crawl glazes, 3 in. (8 cm) in height, 2014. *Image: Courtesy of the artist.*

Volcanic

Volcanic, lava or crater glazes are most commonly made using silicon carbide, which gives off carbon dioxide during firing (6-9). The coarsely ground silicon carbide can be added either to a slip underneath, or to the glaze itself, which should be viscous so that the bubbles burst without healing over.

6-9. Jan Lewin-Cadogan's stoneware bowl, 6 in. (16 cm) in diameter, barium turquoise and lava glaze, fired to 2281°F (1255 °C) in oxidation, 2015. *Image: Courtesy of the artist.*

Crater Glaze
Cone 9

Strontium Carbonate	15%
Nepheline Syenite	61
China Clay	11
Silica	13
	100%

Add:
Silicon Carbide 4%

Luster

Traditional lusters are reduction fired, although modern resin-based lusters can be fired in oxidation, as can a mixture of manganese and copper oxides, which gives a bronze effect (see recipe on page 108). In raku, post-firing reduction is carried out when red-hot pots are removed from the kiln using tongs and covered in sawdust. Copper oxide, tin oxide and silver nitrate can be reduced in these conditions to give metallic effects (6-10).

6-10. Lucie Rie's bowl, 6 in. (15 cm) in diameter, bronze pigment, yellow glaze, private collection. *Image: Henry Bloomfield.*

Bronze Pigment (Steve Ogden)
Cone 2

Copper Oxide	10
Manganese Dioxide	60
China Clay	10
Red Earthenware Clay	20
	100%

Linda Bloomfield, nesting pouring bowls, to 8 in. (20 cm) in diameter, porcelain, praseodymium, copper, cobalt, and nickel oxide glazes, 2013. *Image: Henry Bloomfield.*

CHAPTER 7

Glaze Additives

Glazes are often flocculated to make them thicker and easier to apply. This involves additives that make the clay particles in the glaze stick together in clumps. This is the opposite effect to deflocculation, which is used to make casting slips more fluid. These additives only affect the properties of the glaze while it is in the glaze bucket and during application onto pots. Apart from achieving a more uniform glaze thickness, the effects of the additives during glaze firing are negligible.

FLOCCULATION: CHARGED PARTICLES

Clay particles are in the form of very small hexagonal plate-shaped crystals (see chapter 3 on clay). The edges of the plates have a positive charge and the faces have a negative charge. The edges of one clay particle are attracted to the faces of other particles and a flocculated structure like a house of cards builds up (7-1). This makes the glaze thicker and easier to apply, particularly onto the hard vitrified bisque ware often used in industry. Glazes can be flocculated by adding a small amount of vinegar or calcium chloride to the water in the glaze bucket. Vinegar is an acid, while calcium chloride dissolves in water to form calcium ions and chloride ions, which also act as an acid. Magnesium sulphate (Epsom salts) can be used if the glaze already contains some ball clay or bentonite. The flocculant adds positively charged calcium, Ca^{2+} or magnesium, Mg^{2+} ions, which exchange with the sodium, Na^+ ions on the clay crystal edges and increase their attraction to other clay crystals.

Sometimes glaze materials such as soda feldspar dissolve slightly in the glaze bucket over time and the glaze becomes deflocculated. It will seem thinner and more watered down than when first mixed. Some of the sodium in the feldspar dissolves in the water to become sodium hydroxide, an alkali. When the water becomes alkaline, the clay particles become negatively charged and repel and slide past one other. They settle in layers at the bottom of the glaze bucket, like a flat pack of cards spilled on a table (7-2). Adding acid (or salts which act as acids) to the water overcomes the charge on the clay particles and causes them to attract one another in the house of cards structure. This flocculates the glaze and helps the clay, feldspar, and silica to stay in suspension longer.

Glaze Additives

7-1. Clay particles flocculated (house of cards structure).

7-2. Clay particles deflocculated (flat pack of cards).

If the glaze does not contain enough clay to prevent it settling, it can also be thickened using a gum or cellulose additive such as CMC (carboxy methyl cellulose), which will burn away in the firing.

We have investigated the major components of a glaze: silica, fluxes, and alumina, as well as the ingredients, which make them easier to control when mixed in the glaze bucket. In the next chapter we will look at the changes, which take place during firing, and the different types of kilns used by potters.

CHAPTER 8

Firing

Ceramics must be fired to make them durable. Potters need to know the processes taking place in order to be able to control the outcome. As well as firing the clay, the glaze must also be fired to maturity. It is important to match the firing temperature of the glaze to the maturing temperature for the particular clay body. The type of kiln used and the firing schedule will also have an effect on the color and texture of the glaze.

CERAMIC CHANGE

Clay goes through several physical changes when fired. The first step is the evaporation of water from between the clay particles. Pots must be completely dry before firing, otherwise the steam escaping could cause them to explode. Initially, the kiln should be heated very slowly to give time for all the water to evaporate. Drying can be speeded up by pre-heating the ware in the kiln to 176°F (80°C) for a few hours. This part of the firing, up to 212°F (100°C) is called water smoking, which causes the water in the pores between the clay crystals to evaporate. The next stage is to drive off the water which is chemically combined with the clay (remember the formula for clay is $Al_2O_3 \cdot 2SiO_2 \cdot 2H_2O$). This is known as dehydroxylation and occurs up to 1022°F (550°C). Once this chemical change has taken place, the process cannot be reversed and the clay cannot be returned to its plastic state.

At 1063°F (573°C), the crystalline quartz in the clay body increases in volume by 1% (see silica phases in chapter 6). This may cause cracking if the temperature in the kiln is increased too rapidly. Organic matter in the clay is burned and oxidized to carbon dioxide, and fluorine and sulphur dioxide from materials in the clay body are driven off at 1292–1652°F (700–900°C). At this point the biscuit firing is completed. The clay particles are sintered or welded together. The ware has undergone little shrinkage since the bone-dry stage, but it is durable enough to withstand handling and glazing.

Above 1652°F (900°C), the clay body begins to shrink and vitrify. The silica starts to melt, filling the spaces between the clay particles and fusing them together (8-1 and 8-2). The fired clay is known as metakaolin. At 1832°F (1000°C) the clay crystals begin to break down and melt. At 1922°F (1050°C), needle shaped crystals of mullite $3Al_2O_3 \cdot 2SiO_2$ begin to form, giving the fired clay strength and hardness. When mullite forms from metakaolin $Al_2O_3 \cdot 2SiO_2$, extra free silica is released. Above 2012°F (1100°C), any free silica (not chemically combined) in the clay changes to cristobalite, which has a different structure from that of quartz. When the kiln is cooled down, cristobalite contracts suddenly by 3% at 439°F (226°C) (see silica phases in chapter 6). This can cause cracking if the kiln is cooled too rapidly by opening too soon, causing some areas to drop in temperature and stressing the ware. It is advisable not to open it until it has cooled down to below 212°F (100°C).

8-1. Fired, porous white earthenware, cone 06.   **8-2.** Fired, vitrified porcelain, cone 8.

KILNS

Primitive people probably first carried out firing in bonfires or fire pits. Kilns were eventually enclosed with bricks, either as bottle kilns or, in the Far East, climbing kilns, which were built into hillsides and enabled higher temperatures to be reached. Updraught kilns have the chimney at the top, while cross-draught and downdraught kilns have the flue at the bottom, causing the hot gases to be driven through the ware twice, resulting in a more efficient use of energy.

Kilns can be fired using wood, oil, gas, or electricity. In electric kilns, elements made from a Kanthal A-1 (iron-chromium-aluminium) alloy are heated up by electrical resistance when a current is passed through. In modern electric kilns, the rate of firing can be slowed down by periodically switching the elements on and off. This is carried out by the kiln controller, which can be programmed to fire at a certain rate and to switch the kiln off when the peak temperature is reached. The initial rate of firing can be around 140°F (60°C) per hour for biscuit firing or 212°F (100°C) per hour for glaze firing, increasing to 302°F (150°C) per hour as the firing progresses beyond the critical early stages. Elements will last for 50 firings to cone 10, 100 firings to cone 6 or several hundred firings to cone 06. Electric kiln firings can produce reliable and repeatable results, but any interesting effects rely chiefly on the makeup of the glaze.

Some potters prefer to rely on chance happenings in the wood firing to produce rich surface effects. They may leave the outside of pots unglazed and use the path of the flames, vapors from the wood and fly ash to decorate the surface. There are several types of wood kiln, including the anagama, a single-chambered kiln built on a slope and heated by wood burned in a firebox at the lowest end and by stoking through openings in the sides as the firing progresses (8-3). Multi-chambered climbing kilns are also used, particularly in Japan, although they take longer to fill. Kilns may have separate or integral fireboxes. Wood and gas kilns usually take longer to cool than the more lightweight electric kilns, so there is more chance of surface variegation and crystals forming.

In raku firing, red-hot pots are removed from the kiln at 1652°F (900°C) and buried in sawdust. This enables post-firing reduction of the glaze, often resulting in crazing, metallic luster effects from oxides in the glaze and blackening of unglazed areas. Pots can also be smoke fired by packing in sawdust, setting alight, and leaving until the sawdust is completely burned. Metal salts such as copper sulphate can produce interesting colors.

8-3. John Butler's anagama kiln in Surrey, England.

MEASURING TEMPERATURE

Temperature can be assessed by the color observed through the spy hole, either through a piece of dark glass or welders' goggles.

Red heat 1292–1652°F (700–900°C)
Orange 2012°F (1100°C)
Yellow 2192°F (1200°C)
White 2372°F (1300°C)

A more accurate measure can be made using a pyrometer, connected to a thermocouple probe inside the kiln. The most accurate measure of heat work is made using pyrometric cones made by Seger or Orton (see Appendix 2). These are slender pyramids of glaze material which bend over when a certain amount of heat work has taken place. Heat work depends on the rate of heating, so taking a long time to reach the final temperature will have the same effect on the cone as a shorter time at a higher temperature. Three cones are used, one lower and one higher than the intended firing temperature, for example, cones 7, 8, and 9 are used if the intended firing temperature is cone 8, or 2300°F (1260°C) (8-4). The cones are set in a row at an angle of 8° from the vertical in a pad of clay and placed behind the spy holes in the kiln. They should be set well back from the spy hole. The firing is completed when the central cone tip bends over and touches the base. The guard cone should remain standing to ensure the kiln has not been overfired. Biscuit firing is usually to cone 06 1814°F (990°C), while

8-4. Orton cones before and after firing. In this cone pack, cone 7 is fired to maturity.

glaze firing can be anything between cone 6 and 10 2228–2336°F (1220–1280°C) for stoneware and cone 04 and 02 1940–2012°F (1060–1100°C) for earthenware. Raku firing is to around cone 09, 1652°F 1652°F (900°C), while luster firings are to cone 015, 1472°F (800°C).

OXIDATION AND REDUCTION

In oxidation, there is excess oxygen available, and any iron in the clay body turns buff, or red-brown in the case of red earthenware (containing red iron oxide, Fe_2O_3). In fuel-burning kilns, if there is just sufficient oxygen available for combustion, the atmosphere will be neutral. However, a reduction state can be developed by restricting the air supply, so that there is insufficient oxygen for combustion of the fuel. Oxygen is drawn instead from the clay body and glazes and any iron is reduced to black iron oxide FeO, which acts as a flux. Stoneware clay turns grey, with orange flashing where it comes into contact with sodium from the glaze or vapor from wood or salt in the kiln atmosphere. Classical Chinese glazes need reduction firing to bring out their characteristic colors, including celadon blues, ash glazes, tenmoku, and copper red (8-5). Some glazes developed more recently such as chrome-tin pinks, copper turquoise, and silicon carbide volcanic glazes need an oxidation firing. In general, brighter colors are obtained in oxidation, and more muted, earthy colors in reduction. There is usually more interaction between the body and glaze in reduction, with iron spots in the body bleeding through to the glaze, creating rich glaze effects (8-6). In oxidation, rich effects can be obtained by layering multiple reactive glazes containing coloring oxides.

WOOD AND SALT

Many potters fire using wood for the effects of volatile gases and fly ash, which react with the clay to produce a toasted orange color and drips of molten ash glaze. Flashing slips containing sodium in the form of nepheline syenite can also enhance the orange color from iron oxide in the clay body. These effects can also be produced in sodium vapor glazing, where salt or sodium bicarbonate is introduced into the kiln at high temperature (8-7). The sodium reacts with the silica and alumina in the clay to produce a characteristic orange-peel textured glaze. Color can be introduced using colored slips containing iron, cobalt, and titanium oxides.

8-5. Porcelain bowls by Mirka Golden-Hann: top left oxidized celadon, top right oxidized copper blue, bottom left reduced celadon, and bottom right reduced copper red, fired to cone 9.

Firing

8-6. Matt Fiske's lava oilspot cups, fired to cone 12 in different oxidation and reduction firing cycles, with more than one firing. *Image: Courtesy of the artist.*

8-7. Salt fired porcelain by Susanne Lukács-Ringel, Germany, 2011. *Image: Courtesy of the artist.*

ASH

Wood and grass ash contain the minerals absorbed by the growing plant or tree. These minerals include silica, calcium, magnesium, potassium, sodium, phosphorus, manganese, and iron oxides. Wood ash contains more calcia, while grass ash has more silica (8-8). Bernard Leach classified ashes into hard (grass and straw ash), medium (oak and ash) and soft (apple and beech), depending on the silica content, not the usual meaning of hardwood (deciduous) and softwood (coniferous). The composition of the ash depends on the type of tree, the part of the tree used, whether the bark was included and the season it was cut. Wood ash can be sprinkled directly onto pots, or mixed into a glaze together with feldspar and clay. When fired in reduction, the iron oxide in the ash produces subtle greens, which vary depending on the type of wood, lighter from apple and beech, darker from pine ash. Wood and grass ash can also provide crystallisation and opacity. In oxidation, wood ash melts to a tan yellow glaze, which can be colored green using copper and cobalt oxides.

Ash Glaze (Phil Rogers)
Cone 9 Reduction

Cornwall Stone	14.5%
Whiting	4.5
Wood Ash (unsieved)	53.0
Potash Feldspar	14.5
China Clay	6.5
Silica	7.0
	100.0%

Firing

8-8. Stephen Parry's vase, 10 in. (27 cm) in height stoneware, pine ash glaze: potash feldspar 25, pine ash 35, flint 17, Hyplas 71 ball clay 23, wood fired, 2013. *Image: Courtesy of the artist.*

Wood Ash Analysis

	Ash	Apple	Beech	Oak	Larch	Pine	Spruce	Meadow grass	Wheat straw
Silica SiO_2	24	2	6	10	11	18	4	58	70
Calcia CaO	27	65	56	51	27	32	55	10	6
Potash K_2O	17	15	17	11	21	18	14	15	13
Soda Na_2O	8	6	4	6	9	6	10	4	2
Magnesia MgO	12	6	11	9	8	6	10	5	4
Phosphorus P_2O_5	7	5	5	10	8	7	7	4	5
Iron Fe_2O_3	4	1	1	1	4	4		1	
Manganese MnO_2				1	11	4			
Alumina Al_2O_3	1			1	1	5		3	

8-9. Wood ash analysis. (*Information from* The Potter's Dictionary of Materials and Techniques, *by Frank and Janet Hamer.*)

CONCLUSION

We have learned how chemistry can help potters to understand their materials and how potters' materials can be divided into basic/alkaline fluxes and acid glass formers, which react together in the kiln. Knowledge of geology and how rocks and minerals were formed in the Earth can also help to understand and control what is happening in the kiln. By looking at how the structure of different clays affects their properties, we can select clays appropriate to different making methods and firing temperatures. An understanding of glazes and firing can help potters to produce ceramic surfaces that are both beautiful and functional.

Firing John Butler's anagama, Surrey, UK.

Firing

Matt Fiske's lava oilspot bowls, basalt-rhyolite glaze fired using eight different firing processes with various oxidation and reduction cooling schedules, 2015. *Image: Courtesy of the artist.*

Bibliography

POTTERY
Bloomfield L, *Advanced Pottery,* Crowood Press, 2010.
Cardew M, *Pioneer Pottery*, A&C Black, 2002.
Hamer F and J, *The Potter's Dictionary*, Bloomsbury, 6th edition, 2015.
Obstler M, *Out of the Earth into the Fire*, The American Ceramic Society, 2nd Edition, 2001.
Rhodes D, *Clay and Glazes for the Potter*, A&C Black, 2nd edition, 1973.

SCIENCE
Dawkins R, *The Magic of Reality*, Bantam Press, 2011.
Miodownik M, *Stuff Matters: The Strange Stories of the Marvellous Materials that Shape Our Man-Made World*, Penguin, 2014.

GEOLOGY
British Geological Survey Mineral Planning Factsheet, Ball Clay, 2011.
Fortey R, *The Hidden Landscape, A Journey into the Geological Past*, Pimlico, 1993.
Heathman JH, *Bentonite in Wyoming, Geological Survey of Wyoming*, 1939.
Pellant C, *Rocks and Minerals*, Dorling Kindersley, 1992.
Ries H, *The Clays of the United States East of the Mississippi River*, United States Geological Survey, 1903.

CLAY
Searle AB, *The Natural History of Clay*, Cambridge University Press, 1912.

GLAZE
Ali NJ, *The Chemistry of Ceramic Glazes*, PhD thesis, Aston University, 1983.
Bloomfield L, *Colour in Glazes*, A&C Black and The American Ceramic Society, 2011.
Cooper E and Royle D, *Glazes for the Studio Potter*, Batsford, 1984.
Hesselberth J and Roy R, *Mastering Cone 6 Glazes*, Glaze Master Press, 2002.
Jernegan J, *Dry Glazes*, University of Pennsylvania Press, 2009.
Rogers P, *Ash Glazes*, A&C Black, 1991.
Taylor B and Doody K, *Glaze: The Ultimate Ceramic Artist's Guide to Glaze and Color*, Quarto, 2014.
Taylor JR and Bull AC, *Ceramics Glaze Technology*, Pergamon Press, 1986.

HISTORY
Davis EE, *Industrial History*, Oak Hill, Ohio, 1980.

Science for Potters

Glossary

acid A non-metal oxide, which when dissolved in water, releases hydrogen ions H⁺.

alkali The oxide of an alkali metal or alkaline earth metal, which when dissolved in water, releases hydroxide ions OH⁻.

alkali metals Metals in the first column of the periodic table: lithium, sodium, and potassium.

alkaline earths Metals in the second column of the periodic table: magnesium, calcium, strontium, and barium.

alkaline frit A frit containing sodium, potassium, and silica.

alkaline glaze Glaze high in sodium, lithium, potassium, strontium, or barium.

amphoteric Able to act either as an acid or as a base/alkali.

atom The smallest unit of matter.

ball clay Fine-grained, plastic, secondary clay.

ball mill A rotating drum containing ceramic pebbles for grinding coloring oxides in glazes.

base A metal oxide, which does not dissolve in water but will react with an acid.

basalt A fine-grained, dark volcanic rock containing iron and magnesium.

bentonite A very plastic secondary clay, used to suspend glazes.

biscuit firing A first firing, usually to around 1832°F (1000°C), done before applying a glaze.

blistering Blisters in a fired glaze caused by gas escaping during firing.

bloating Blisters in the clay body, caused by trapped bubbles of gas.

borax frit A frit containing sodium, calcium, boron, and silica.

calcine To heat materials in a kiln to drive off volatile compounds.

celadon A type of pale, gray-green or blue-green glaze containing iron oxide.

china clay Kaolin, pure white clay.

chun A pale blue, opalescent glaze.

close-packed Crystal structure in which the atoms are packed as densely as possible.

CMC Carboxymethyl cellulose gum, used to suspend glaze ingredients in water.
cone A small, slender pyramid of glaze material, set in the kiln, which bends over when fired to the correct temperature.
Cornwall stone A type of feldspar found in Cornwall, UK.
covalent bonding When atoms bond together by sharing electrons.
crawling A defect where glaze pulls away from the body, leaving bare patches.
crazing A network of fine cracks caused by a higher coefficient of expansion in the glaze than in the clay body.
cristobalite A crystalline form of silica, which forms in the clay body above 2012°F (1100°C) and contracts suddenly on cooling at 439°F (226°C).
crystalline A glaze in which crystals have grown during cooling.
devitrify The growth of crystals from the molten glaze, which is then no longer in the glassy state.
dunting Cracking caused by cold air entering the kiln during cooling.
earthenware Fired to a low temperature, below 2102°F (1150°C), where the clay body remains porous.
electron Small, negatively-charged particle inside the atom.
element A single type of atom.
eutectic The lowest melting combination of two or more materials.
feldspar A mineral composed of potassium, sodium, or calcium alumino-silicate crystals.
felsic Light-colored rock or mineral containing feldspar and silica.
flashing Color resulting from volatile compounds released during firing.
flocculate To cause glaze particles to clump together and thicken the glaze.
flux A material that lowers the melting temperature of a glaze.
frit Glaze fluxes melted with silica and sometimes alumina, and ground to a powder.
granite A medium-grained, igneous rock composed of feldspar, quartz, and mica.
hydroxyl A group with an oxygen atom connected by a covalent bond to a hydrogen atom.
igneous Rocks formed from cooled magma.
illite A common type of secondary clay derived from mica.

ion An atom or molecule, which has lost or gained an electron.
ionic When atoms bond by transferring electrons from one to the other.
kaki A red-brown, high-iron glaze. Kaki is the Japanese word for persimmon.
kaolinite A pure, white clay mineral.
luster Metallic decoration obtained by reducing metal salts.
mafic Dark rock or mineral containing magnesium and iron.
magma Molten rock.
marl A type of earthenware clay high in calcium.
metamorphic Rocks formed from other rocks by pressure or heat.
mica A lustrous, platy mineral.
mineral An inorganic substance with an ordered atomic structure, e.g. quartz.
molecule Two or more atoms bonded together with no overall charge.
molochite Finely-ground, calcined china clay.
neutron Particle in the nucleus of the atom which has no charge.
nuka A Japanese glaze made from rice-hull ash.
octahedron Solid shape with six corners and eight triangular faces.
opacifier A material that does not dissolve in a glaze, causing it to become opaque.
orbitals Regions in which electrons of a particular energy spin around the nucleus of an atom.
oxidation Firing in the presence of sufficient oxygen, usually in an electric kiln.
oxide An element bound to oxygen.
pinholes Small holes in a glaze, caused by burst bubbles that have not healed over during firing.
porcelain A white clay body fired to 2282–2552°F (1250–1400°C), becoming translucent and vitrified.
proton Positively charged particle in the nucleus of the atom.
pyrometer A device used to measure the temperature inside a kiln.
raku Low-temperature firing where red hot pots are removed from the kiln.
reduction The act of limiting the air available during firing, so that oxygen is drawn from the clay and glaze.
refractory Able to withstand high temperatures.
rhyolite A fine-grained, light-colored volcanic rock high in silica.

rock An aggregate of minerals, e.g. granite.
salt firing Introducing salt into the kiln at high temperatures to combine with silica in the clay and produce a glaze on the surface.
sedimentary Rocks formed from deposited layers of sediment.
shino A white Japanese glaze made from feldspar and clay.
shivering Glaze flaking off at rims and edges of handles, caused by poor glaze fit with the glaze contracting less than the clay body.
silica Silicon dioxide, found in quartz, flint, or sand.
slip Clay mixed with water.
soak To maintain the top firing temperature to mature the glaze evenly throughout the kiln.
soda firing Introducing soda (sodium carbonate) into the kiln at high temperatures to combine with silica in the clay to produce a glaze on the surface.
spinel Stable, close-packed cubic structure with the formula $MgAl_2O_4$, used for ceramic stains. The magnesium and aluminium in the formula can be replaced with coloring oxides such as iron, cobalt, and chromium.
stain Industrially-produced ceramic pigment containing coloring oxides and opacifiers.
stoneware Fired to a high temperature, above 2192°F (1200°C), so that the clay body is vitrified and non-porous.
tenmoku A brown-black, high-iron glaze.
tetrahedron Triangle-based pyramid with four corners and four triangular faces.
transition metal Element with an incomplete inner electron shell.
valence The combining power of an element. The number of hydrogen atoms it will combine with.
vitrify To fire to a glassy state.

Appendices

Appendix 1: Ceramic Materials List

Ceramic materials, chemical formulae, and molecular or equivalent* weights (containing one molecule).

Material	Formula	Molecular Weight
Alumina	Al_2O_3	102
Alumina hydrate	$Al(OH)_3$	78*
Barium carbonate	$BaCO_3$	197.3
Bentonite	$Al_2O_3 \cdot 4SiO2 \cdot H_2O$	360.3
Bone ash (calcium phosphate)	$Ca_3(PO_4)_2$	103*
Borax	$Na_2O \cdot 2B_2O_3 \cdot 10H_2O$	381.4
Boric oxide	B_2O_3	69.6
Calcium borate	$Ca(BO_2)_2$	125.7
Cerium oxide	CeO_2	172.1
China clay	$Al_2O_3 \cdot 2SiO_2 \cdot 2H_2O$	258.2
Colemanite	$2CaO \cdot 3B_2O_3 \cdot 5H_2O$	206*
Cornwall stone	$K_2O.Al_2O_3 \cdot 8SiO_2$	676.8
Chromium oxide	Cr_2O_3	152
Cobalt carbonate	$CoCO_3$	119
Cobalt oxide	CoO	74.9
Copper oxide	CuO	79.5
Cryolite	Na_3AlF_6	210
Dolomite	$CaCO_3 \cdot MgCO_3$	184.4
Erbium oxide	Er_2O_3	382.5
Feldspar soda (albite)	$Na_2O \cdot Al_2O_3 \cdot 6SiO_2$	524.4
Feldspar potash (orthoclase)	$K_2O \cdot Al_2O_3 \cdot 6SiO_2$	556.4

Material	Formula	Mol. Wt.
Feldspar lime (anorthite)	CaO·Al$_2$O$_3$·2SiO$_2$	278.2
Fluorspar	CaF$_2$	78.1
Ilmenite	FeO·TiO$_2$	151.7
Iron (ferric) oxide (red)	Fe$_2$O$_3$	159.7
Iron (ferrous) oxide (black)	FeO	71.8
Kaolin	Al$_2$O$_3$·2SiO$_2$·2H$_2$O	258.2
Kyanite	Al$_2$O$_3$·SiO$_2$	162
Lead bisilicate	PbO·2SiO$_2$	343.4
Lead oxide (litharge)	PbO	223.2
Lead sulphide (galena)	PbS	239.2
Lead sesquisilicate	2PbO·3SiO$_2$	313.3*
Lepidolite	LiF·KF·Al$_2$O$_3$·3SiO$_2$	366.3
Lithium carbonate	Li$_2$CO$_3$	73.9
Magnesia	MgO	40.3
Magnesium carbonate	MgCO$_3$	84.3
Manganese dioxide	MnO$_2$	87
Mullite	3Al$_2$O$_3$·2SiO$_2$	426.1
Neodymium oxide	Nd$_2$O$_3$	336.5
Nepheline syenite	K$_2$O·3Na$_2$O·4Al$_2$O$_3$·8SiO$_2$	389.6*
Nickel oxide	NiO	74.7
Petalite	Li$_2$O·Al$_2$O$_3$·8SiO$_2$	612.5
Praseodymium oxide	Pr$_2$O$_3$	329.8
Quartz	SiO$_2$	60.1
Rutile	TiO$_2$	79.9
Silicon carbide	SiC	40.1
Silica	SiO$_2$	60.1
Spinel	MgAl$_2$O$_4$	142.3

Spodumene	$Li_2O \cdot Al_2O_3 \cdot 4SiO_2$	372.2
Strontium carbonate	$SrCO_3$	147.6
Talc (magnesium silicate)	$3MgO \cdot 4SiO_2 \cdot H_2O$	126.4*
Tin oxide	SnO_2	150.7
Titanium oxide (anatase)	TiO_2	79.9
Vanadium pentoxide	V_2O_5	181.9
Whiting (calcium carbonate)	$CaCO_3$	100.1
Wollastonite (calcium silicate)	$CaSiO_3$	116.2
Zinc oxide	ZnO	81.4
Zirconium silicate	$ZrSiO_4$	183.3

*Equivalent weights (containing one molecule) are sometimes given where the chemical formula contains a multiple number of molecules, for example, talc contains three molecules of magnesia, so the total molecular weight is divided by three to give the equivalent weight of talc containing one molecule of magnesia.

Appendix 2: Orton Pyrometric Cone Temperatures

Pyrometric cones measure heat work, and so they depend on the heating rate. A slower temperature rise will cause the cone to bend at a lower temperature.

Cone no.	60°C/hour	108°F/hour	150°C/hour	270°F/hour
09	917	1683	928	1702
08	942	1728	954	1749
07	973	1783	984	1805
06	995	1823	985	1852
05	1030	1886	1046	1915
04	1060	1940	1070	1958
03	1086	1987	1101	2014
02	1101	2014	1120	2048
01	1117	2043	1137	2079
1	1136	2077	1154	2109
2	1142	2088	1162	2124
3	1152	2106	1168	2134
4	1160	2120	1181	2158
5	1184	2163	1205	2201
6	1220	2228	1241	2266
7	1237	2259	1255	2291
8	1247	2277	1269	2316
9	1257	2295	1278	2332
10	1282	2340	1303	2377
11	1293	2359	1312	2394
12	1304	2379	1324	2415
13	1321	2410	1346	2455
14	1388	2530	1366	2491

Appendix 3: Phase Diagram for Silica-Alumina-Calcia

The contour lines show temperature (blue is relatively cool, red, and yellow are hot). The eutectic point is the lowest melting combination at 2138°F (1170°C). Lime is calcium oxide; wollastonite is calcium silicate, corundum is alumina, mullite is alumina-silicate, cristobalite and tridymite are silica phases, and anorthite is calcium feldspar. Note: The contour lines show temperature in °C.

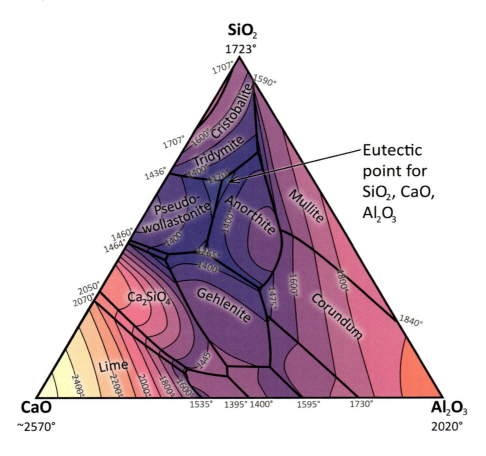

Appendix 4: Materials Analysis for US Frits, Clays, and Feldspars

	K_2O	Na_2O	Li_2O	BaO	CaO	MgO	ZnO	Al_2O_3	B_2O_3	SiO_2	Mol. wt.
Ferro Frit 3110	.060	.650			.290			.095	.097	3.029	260
Ferro Frit 3124	.021	.282			.698			.269	.519	2.554	275
Ferro Frit 3134		.317			.683				.633	1.890	191
Ferro Frit 3195		.336			.654	.01		.392	1.136	2.656	337
Ferro Frit 3249					.171	.829		.357	1.137	1.919	274

Clays and Feldspars, percentage composition (LOI = loss on ignition)

	SiO_2	TiO_2	Al_2O_3	Fe_2O_3	P_2O_5	CaO	MgO	K_2O	Na_2O	LOI
EPK	45.91	.34	38.71	0.42		0.09	.12	.22	.04	14.15
Georgia Kaolin	45.20	1.95	38.02	0.49		0.26	.30	.04	.02	13.72
OM 4 Ball Clay	55.20	1.20	29.70	1.10		0.30	.40	1.00	.30	12.60
Custer Feldspar	68.50		17.50	0.08		0.30	.01	10.40	3.00	0.21
G-200 Feldspar	65.76		19.28	0.06		0.98	.01	10.36	3.20	0.35
Kona F-4 Feldspar	66.77		19.59	0.04		1.70	.01	4.50	7.00	0.39
NC-4 Feldspar	68.81		18.74	0.07		1.60	.01	3.76	6.89	0.12
Tennessee No.5 Ball Clay	53.30	1.40	31.10	1.00		0.30	.20	1.50	0.80	10.40

Appendix 5: Materials Analysis for UK Frits, Clays, and Feldspars

	K$_2$O	Na$_2$O	Li$_2$O	BaO	CaO	MgO	ZnO	Al$_2$O$_3$	B$_2$O$_3$	SiO$_2$	Mol. wt.
Calcium Borate Frit	0.01				0.99	0.01		0.1	1.5	0.62	209
Standard Borax Frit	0.04	0.35			0.61	0.01		0.18	0.62	1.98	240
High-Alkaline Frit	0.21	0.59	0.01	0.09	0.1			0.1	0.1	1.71	196
Low-Expansion Frit	0.03	0.2			0.76	0.01		0.55	1.02	3.39	390

Clays and Feldspars, percentage composition (LOI = loss on ignition)

	SiO$_2$	TiO$_2$	Al$_2$O$_3$	Fe$_2$O$_3$	P$_2$O$_5$	CaO	MgO	K$_2$O	Na$_2$O	LOI
China Clay	48.8	0.1	35.4	0.8				1.6	1.5	11.8
AT Ball Clay	54	1.1	29	2.4		0.3	0.4	3	0.5	9.3
HP71 Ball Clay	70	1.6	19	0.8		0.2	0.4	2	0.5	5.5
HV AR Ball Clay	60.3	1.5	26.7	0.9		0.2	0.3	2.6	0.4	7.1
Cornish Stone	73.2	0.06	15.3	0.13	0.47	1.47	0.13	4.45	3.44	1.35
Nepheline Syenite	60.5		23	0.1		1		5	10.2	0.2
Potash Feldspar	65.8		18.5	0.1		0.38		12	2.89	0.33
Soda Feldspar	67.9		19	0.11		1.88		2.8	7.5	0.81
FFF Feldspar	67.7		18.9	0.16		0.72		7.62	4.85	0.05

Appendix 6: Complete Periodic Table of Elements

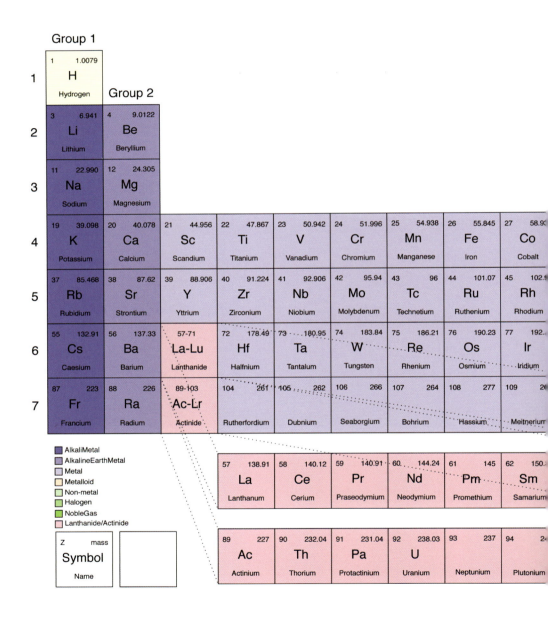

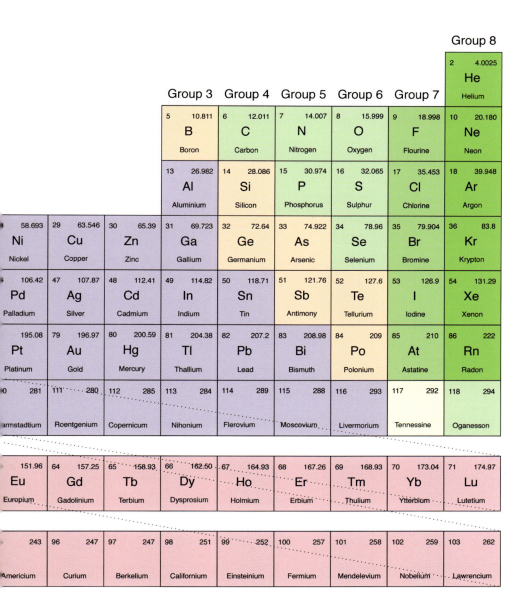

Index

acidic	24, 31
alkali metals	25
alkaline	6, 24
alkaline earth	26
alumina	30, 58
amphoteric	24, 90
antimony	23
ash glaze	120
atom	2
ball clay	51, 69
barium	26, 57, 90
basalt	40, 41
base	1, 24
bentonite	38, 49, 77, 78
bisque	113
blistering	101
bonding	5
bonding: covalent	5
bonding: ionic	5, 7
bone ash	55, 74
borax frit	65, 92
boron	23, 30, 57
calcium	55
carbon	31, 69
Carboniferous	45
celadon	55, 70
chemical formula	4, 89
china clay	68

chrome-tin pink	62, 117
chromium oxide	27, 62
clay	67
clay body	72
clay structure	75, 77
close-packed structure	8, 12
cobalt carbonate	59
cobalt oxide	16, 27, 59
coefficient of expansion	100
color	13, 14
coloring oxides	27, 59
cones	116
copper oxide	17, 27, 62
Cornwall stone	48, 54
corundum	10, 14, 30
crater glaze	106
crawling	100
crazing	98
Cretaceous	49
cristobalite	97
crystal field theory	20
crystal structure	7, 9, 11
crystalline glaze	103
crystals	7, 9
deflocculation	110
devitrification	104
dolomite	55
dunting	72, 97
earthenware	71, 72, 74, 117
electric kiln	114
element	2
eutectic	26, 31, 82, 84
expansion	100

feldspar	39, 48, 53
felsic	37, 39
fireclay	45
firing	113
firing: wood	115, 117
firing: oxidation	117
firing: raku	115
firing: reduction	117
firing: salt	117
firing: soda	117
flint	57
flocculation	70, 110
flux	25, 36, 33
frit	57
fumes	72
gas kiln	114
gemstones	14, 27
geology	36
glaze	81
glaze faults	98
glaze fit	97
glaze formula	90
glaze recipe	89
glaze stains	18
glaze structure	85
glaze: ash glaze	120
glaze: bronze	108
glaze: celadon	117
glaze: chun	104
glaze: crackle	98
glaze: crater	106
glaze: crystalline	103
glaze: earthenware	82, 92, 100

glaze: lichen	106
glaze: limits for stable	94
glaze: material substitution	90, 92
glaze: matte	102
granite	37, 41
hardness	12
history	44, 48
illite	39, 71, 78
ilmenite	63
interstitial	11
iron oxide	27, 62
Jurassic	49
kaolin	67, 76
kiln	114
kiln: electric	114
kiln: gas	114
kyanite	13, 58
lead	30
lime matte	84
limestone	55, 56
lithium	25, 51
luster	107
mafic	37, 39
magnesium	26
manganese dioxide	27, 62
marl	48
matte glaze	102
melting point	25, 33
metals	23, 25
mica	39, 41, 71, 79
minerals	51
molecular weight	90
molecule	4

molochite	72
mullite	8, 82, 113
natron	3
nepheline syenite	55
nickel oxide	27, 63
opacifier	63
orbitals	2, 18, 19
oxide	32
periodic table	22
phase diagram	82, 83
phosphorus	32
pinholes	101
porcelain	72
potassium	25
pyrometer	116
pyroxene	37, 38, 104
quartz	10, 97
rare earth oxides	28, 29
reduction	117
refractory	72
rhyolite	40, 41
rocks	37
ruby	14
rutile	63
salt glaze	117
satin matte	103
Seger, Hermann	116
semiconductors	30, 31
shale	44
shivering	99
silica	5, 39, 58, 85, 97
slip	69, 117
soda glaze	117

sodium	25
spinel	12
stains	18
stoneware	49, 74
strontium	26, 57, 90
surface tension	101
talc	44
tenmoku	117
thermocouple	116
tin oxide	30, 63, 64
titanium	27, 63
transition metal	27
transparent glaze	84, 89
units	8
uranium oxide	29
valence	1, 6
vanadium	27, 63
vitrification	74, 113
whiting	55
willemite	104
wood ash	120
zinc oxide	28, 57
zirconium	63

© Linda Bloomfield, 2017

Appendix